MW00767966

Peach State Paradise

A flagstone pathway (previous page,
left) meanders through Founders
Memorial Garden in Athens.

A flower spider (previous page,
right) moves slowly across a
dew-covered morning glory.

PEACH STATE PARADISE
A Guide to Gardens and Natural Areas of Georgia

Photographs by AL SPICER

Text by CINDY SPICER

John F. Blair, Publisher
Winston-Salem,
North Carolina

PRINTED AND BOUND IN CHINA

DESIGNED BY LIZA LANGRALL

*The paper in this book meets the guidelines
for permanence and durability of the
Committee on Production Guidelines
for Book Longevity of the Council on
Library Resources.*

Library of Congress Cataloging-in-Publication Data
Spicer, Al, 1950-
     Peach state paradise : a guide to gardens and natural areas of
Georgia / photographs by Al Spicer ; text by Cindy Spicer.
          p.   cm.
     Includes bibliographical references (p.   ) and index.
     ISBN 0-89587-206-4 (alk. paper)
          1. Gardens—Georgia—Guidebooks.   2. Natural areas—Georgia—Guidebooks.
     3. Gardens—Georgia—Pictorial works.   4. Natural areas—Georgia—Pictorial works.
     5. Georgia—Guidebooks.
     I. Spicer, Cindy, 1954-   .   II. Title.
     SB466.U65G48   1997
     917.580443—dc21   97-22003

DEDICATION

To my big sister, Cathie,
who protected me when I was little,
and to my little brother, Chris,
on whom I picked until he got bigger than me

To my grandmother, Cleo F. Hogan,
who loves God, roses, petunias,
and all of her twenty-two grandchildren

CONTENTS

High Wire, by Victor Salmones, is one of several statues placed throughout Atlanta Botanical Garden.

A folded-winged skipper
gathers nectar from a
globe amaranth.

ACKNOWLEDGMENTS

This book would not have been possible without the people who created Georgia's gardens, and for their work we are grateful. Our thanks go to those who arranged for us to photograph the gardens, especially Olivia Alison, Owens-Thomas House of the Telfair Museum of Art; Dr. Richard Betterly, Isaiah Davenport House Museum; Stephen Bohlin-Davis, Juliette Gordon Low Birthplace; Scott Breithaupt, Oak Hill at the Martha Berry Museum; Laurel Davis, Vines Botanical Gardens; Henry "Bo" Edwards, Lockerly Arboretum; John Gibson, Georgia Southern Botanical Garden; Dr. Michael Guido, Guido Gardens; Pauline Holloway, Barnsley Gardens at Woodlands; Betty Hotchkiss, Massee Lane Gardens; Lisa Littlefield, Atlanta History Center; Laura Anne Middlesteadt, Atlanta Botanical Garden; Angela Moody, Callaway Gardens; and Shelda Rees, Rock City Gardens.

The following people provided us with invaluable information: Betty Arnold, Andrew Low House; Glenn Austin, Antique Rose Emporium; Karin Bennedsen, Panola Mountain State Conservation Park; Lavon Callahan, Elachee Nature Science Center; Marcia Daniels, William H. Reynolds Nature Preserve; Deron Davis, Dunwoody Nature Center; Ike English, Dauset Trails Nature Center; Greg Greer, Chattahoochee Nature Center; Susan Grooms, The Crescent; Frances Hale, Atlanta History Center; Dr. Robert Hayward, Fernbank Science Center; Valerie Hinesley, Hinesley and Associates; Katherine Keena, Juliette Gordon Low Birthplace; Monica Kilpatrick, Cochran Mill Nature Center and Arboretum; Patti King of Savannah; Mark Lamade, Oak Hill at the Martha Berry Museum; Jeanne Lehmann; Jill Lemke, Birdsong Nature Center; Karen Menton, Chattahoochee Nature Center; Sarah Query, Coastal Gardens; George Sanko, DeKalb College Botanical Gardens; Claudia Severin, The Crescent; Barry Smith, city of Augusta; Hilda Thomason, Fred Hamilton Rhododendron Garden; Mona Trotter, Thomas County Library; Charlotte Turner, Cator Woolford Gardens; John Watkins, Oak Hill at the Martha Berry Museum; Karen Wiedmeier, Augusta Public Library; and Lila Williams, Guido Gardens.

We also thank our friends Bill Bailey, for suggestions and comic relief; Dennis and Suzy Bridges, for their support and e-mail; Steve House, who kept us from becoming hermits; Robert and Gloria Johnson, for their encouragement and dinner; Gwen and Wally Luebke, for helping to identify the mystery plants we often encountered; and Mom and Dad, for everything.

Finally, we would like to thank the people at John F. Blair, Publisher, especially Carolyn Sakowski, Liza Langrall, and Steve Kirk, for their continued support and expertise.

Rock City's Swing-Along Bridge at
Lookout Mountain provides spectacular
views of the autumn color.

INTRODUCTION

Gardens and natural areas are becoming more important as they assume the role of surrogate backyard for many individuals. These areas have a universal appeal for gardeners, nature lovers, and anyone interested in either the cultivated curves of a well-executed landscape plan or the natural tangle of wild and protected nature. Garden travel is an affordable pastime enjoyed by millions of people. Georgia beckons plant connoisseurs and lovers of bygone days to its gardens, part of a rich Southern horticultural heritage that traces its roots to the first settlement in Savannah and continues to flourish in the fertile ground of the New South. Noted for its beautiful private gardens, Georgia also boasts spectacular public gardens waiting for you to wander their pathways.

If you have no time to slip away from the rigors of work, then lose yourself in the photographs of some of the Southeast's premier botanical treasures. The photographs in *Peach State Paradise* reveal the gardens in all their floral glory by showing their changing moods, textures, and layers. Look closely and imagine enjoying the delights of a simple fragrance garden, reminiscing in an old rose garden, or wandering slowly through a wonderland of native wildflowers. Embrace each garden and allow it to touch you and provide you with a personal gardening experience as nature's handiwork is revealed one page after another. Watch as the gardens rejoice at winter's passing with an abundance of spring blooms and as they eventually and colorfully fade into another season.

Visiting the gardens vicariously is one way to enjoy the horticultural beauty awaiting you in Georgia. The best way, however, is to visit the gardens with *Peach State Paradise* as your guide. It's wise to do as much pre-trip planning as possible. In *Peach State Paradise*, we've helped to eliminate unknown factors, thereby allowing you to concentrate on enjoying your visit to the fullest. You may also wish to obtain a current state or city map. Directions given for each garden are fairly specific, but mileages are only an approximation. If you plan to visit several gardens in an area, you'll appreciate the side-trip information. Also, call your intended destination to inquire about local lodging. Reservations are recommended, as the excitement of spur-of-the-moment travel wears off quickly when you find yourself sleeping in your car. Here's to happy and safe traveling in Peach State paradise.

The traditional Japanese Garden is
one of the many specialty gardens at
Atlanta Botanical Garden.

GEORGIA

1. Adairsville
2. Athens
3. Atlanta
4. Augusta
5. Dahlonega
6. Decatur
7. Dunwoody
8. Fairburn
9. Fort Valley
10. Gainesville
11. Hampton
12. Hiawassee
13. Jackson
14. Loganville
15. Lookout Mountain
16. Metter
17. Milledgeville
18. Morrow
19. Mount Berry
20. Pine Mountain
21. Roswell
22. Savannah
23. Statesboro
24. Stockbridge
25. Thomasville
26. Valdosta

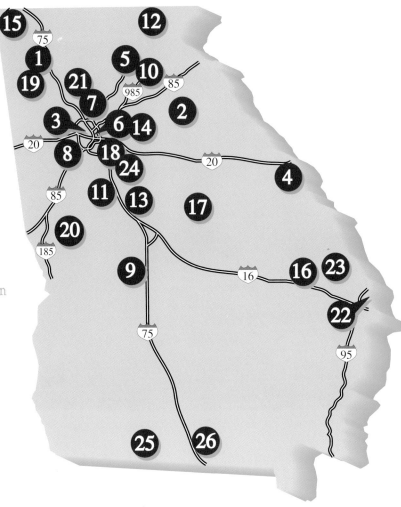

The trails and pathways at Barnsley Gardens at Woodlands take the visitor through a variety of natural and man-made gardens.

BARNSLEY GARDENS
AT WOODLANDS

Address

597 Barnsley Gardens Road
Adairsville, Georgia 30103-5712
770-773-7480

Hours

From January 1 to June 30, the gardens are open Tuesday through Sunday from 10:00 a.m. to 6:00 p.m. From July 1 to December 31, they are open Tuesday through Sunday from 10:00 a.m to 5:00 p.m. The restaurant is open from 11:30 a.m. to 3:00 p.m.

Fees

Yes. Some discounts apply. Children under twelve are admitted free with a paying adult.

History

It is almost impossible to resist the temptation to begin the intricate and tragic story of Godfrey Barnsley and his beloved Julia with any words other than "Once upon a time . . ." The Barnsleys' story began in 1824, when young Godfrey arrived in the United States from Great Britain at age eighteen with little more than the clothes on his back and ambition. In ten short years, he became one of the wealthiest cotton merchants in Savannah.

A very eligible bachelor at twenty-eight, he set his sights on Julia Scarborough of Savannah. In 1828, after overcoming her father's objections, the two were married. The newlyweds remained in Savannah for a short time before Godfrey, anxious to sever the strangling ties of Julia's mother, moved Julia and their budding family to England. Eventually, Julia and the children returned to Savannah and enjoyed everything city life had to offer: parties, teas, tableaux, and lavish balls.

In 1841, the family moved to the northwest Georgia mountains, where Godfrey had begun building Woodlands Manor. He never cared for the term *plantation* and always referred to his

thirty-five-hundred-acre mountain home as a *manor*. In a makeshift cottage which was later to become the cook's wing, the Barnsley family—Godfrey, Julia, and eight children—made the best of frontier living. Life was difficult during the first years at Woodlands. Julia, whose health had never been robust, began to decline due to tuberculosis. In 1845, after recovering in Savannah from a short illness, she died unexpectedly. She was buried in the family vault of friends, never to return to her husband, her family, or Woodlands Manor. After her death, Godfrey began a lifelong infatuation with spiritualism, claiming even to speak with Julia in the boxwood garden in front of the unfinished Woodlands Manor. He continued the work on the house with help and guidance from Julia's ghost, whom he consulted on numerous occasions as work on the estate progressed.

The landscaping of the estate may have been directed by the ghost of Julia Barnsley, but the real genius behind the spirit was Andrew Jackson Downing. Today, Barnsley Gardens at Woodlands is the only testament to Downing's

Adjacent to the ruins of Woodlands Manor is the cook's wing, which once served as the Barnsleys' home. It is now a museum.

work that survives in the South. Downing, it is believed, may never have set foot on the grounds at Woodlands Manor. However, Godfrey Barnsley relied heavily on Downing's landscaping manuals in designing the estate's gardens and natural areas.

Barnsley, the successful cotton merchant, was able to amass quite a collection of plants from around the world by having the captains of his ships fill plant requests. These plants were brought to Woodlands Manor, where Barnsley began filling the countryside with a profusion of beauty. The estate impressed a Union general so much during Georgia's occupation by Northern troops that he ordered his men not to damage the property. Barnsley's estate was spared during the savagery of the Civil War, but his fortune was not. He was so heavily invested in the Confederacy, even turning his fleet of merchant ships over to its navy, that he was brought to financial ruin at the war's end, and the manor house was left unfinished.

History buffs and gardeners looking for a weekend getaway will find plenty to pique their interest at Barnsley Gardens.

Barnsley Gardens features a Chinese fir believed to be the largest in the United States and the 150-year-old Boxwood Parterre.

In 1873, Godfrey Barnsley died with only the clothes on his back and memories of his beloved Julia and Woodlands. He left the property to his children. In 1906, the unfinished and deteriorating house was devastated by a tornado. Time and disrepair then began to return the house to the earth. In 1975, the property was added to the National Register of Historic Places. The designation, however, wasn't enough to stem the tide of decay.

Fortunately, Barnsley Gardens at Woodlands was purchased by Prince Hubertus Fugger and Princess Alexandra of Germany in 1988. The prince and princess began to remove more than a century of dust and decay from the face of the once-magnificent estate. Dedicated to historic preservation, the Fuggers have rejuvenated, preserved, and/or restored the existing buildings on the estate. They have also saved other structures from around the state of Georgia and brought them here, where, like Godfrey, they will find eternal peace in the Woodlands.

Size

1,200 acres, with 30 acres of preserved and restored historical gardens from the mid-1800s

Features

Barnsley Gardens at Woodlands can boast romance as one of its many features. The manor house ruins have been preserved rather than restored, allowing the visitor's imagination to take flight back to antebellum times. The Boxwood Parterre, planted by Godfrey Barnsley and referred to by him as "The Oval," has been restored to its former splendor, complete with a replica of the original fountain. Other horticultural features include the Rose Garden, the

Perennial Border (the final resting place for a Confederate soldier), and more than half a million daffodils, which burst upon the rolling hillsides at the first hint of spring. Closely following the daffodils are the native Georgia wildflowers, which bloom in the Wildflower Meadow throughout the spring and summer. Other features are George's Cotton Patch; the Arbor, which features roses; the Rock Gardens; the Azalea Walk, lined with native azaleas; the Bog Garden; the Lily Pond; the Pinetum and Conifer Collection; and the Heirloom Orchard.

Directions

From I-75, take Exit 128 (GA 140) and travel west for 1.6 miles to Hall Station Road. Turn left, travel 5.3 miles to Barnsley Gardens Road, turn right, and travel 2.4 miles. The entrance to the gardens is on the left.

Tips

Prior to your trip to the gardens, write for a schedule of activities. If possible, start your garden visit early and make arrangements for a tour. Tours are led by a knowledgeable volunteer at no charge or by a staff historian or horticulturist (depending upon your area of interest) for a modest fee. Once the tour is over, wander the grounds and explore the ruins to absorb the ambiance. Regardless of your reason for visiting the gardens, plan to enjoy the lunch buffet at

the Barnsley Gardens Restaurant. Southern cuisine, the real thing, is revisited with flair and generosity. You will not be disappointed. Collectors of heirloom plants, garden tools, and gardening books will discover many treasures at the Plant Shop. The Red House Gift Shop carries a wide variety of gift items for family and friends.

Accessibility

The pathways at the gardens are gravel. Some individuals may require assistance. All public restrooms are accessible to the disabled, as are parts of the museum and ruins. Assistance is available by arrangement.

Cosmos, one of the perennials in the Heirloom Herbaceous Border, are mirrored in raindrops.

Side Trips

Oak Hill at the Martha Berry Museum (pages 106–11) is 20 miles southwest of Adairsville and just north of Rome. Rock City Gardens (pages 86–93) is in Lookout Mountain, 70 miles northwest of Adairsville and about 5 miles south of the Tennessee border.

FOUNDERS MEMORIAL GARDEN

Address

The Garden Club of Georgia, Inc.
State Headquarters House
325 South Lumpkin Street
Athens, Georgia 30602-1865
706-542-3631

Hours

The garden is open year-round from sunrise to sunset. The museum house is open for tours by appointment. The office is open Monday through Friday from 9:00 a.m. to noon and from 1:00 p.m. to 4:00 p.m. and is closed on Saturday, Sunday, and most major holidays.

Fees

Donations are accepted.

History

The year 1891 was a red-letter year for American gardening, as twelve women organized and founded the nation's first garden club, the Ladies Garden Club of Athens. In 1936, the State Garden Club established a fund to create an appropriate memorial to the founders. Ten years later, Founders Memorial Garden was completed. The garden, a living monument to these women, is located on the campus of the University of Georgia. It was designed under the direction of Hubert Owens, founder and head of the University of Georgia's Department of Landscape Architecture in the 1940s. Owens coordinated the efforts of his staff and students along with resources from the Garden Club of Georgia to design and develop the garden, which was completed in 1946.

The garden surrounds the Garden Club of Georgia State Headquarters, which moved to the site in 1961. Prior to becoming the club's headquarters, the house, built in 1857, was used by the university in various capacities. Just after it was built, the two-story house with detached kitchen and smokehouse was used as a residence

for professors. Later, it was used as a dining hall, then as a biological science building. During its tenure as the science building, it was dubbed the "Rat House" by students, as the kitchen was used to house laboratory rats. When the house

The Lenten rose, a member of the hellebore family, is among the first plants to bloom in the spring.

was no longer needed as a science laboratory, it became the residence of the first dean of women. Upon her death, the Phi Mu sorority had its chapter there. Later, the old house provided quarters for the Department of Landscape Architecture. In 1961, the complex of buildings was no longer needed by the university, and permission was granted to the State Garden Club to use the house and support buildings as its permanent headquarters.

Founders Memorial Garden has evolved into one of the university's most treasured and useful assets, serving not only as a living laboratory for students majoring in landscape architecture, ornamental horticulture, and botany, but also as

The Formal Boxwood Garden is designed in the traditional pattern of a circular clipped hedge.

Various species of brightly colored flowers paint the landscape around Founders Memorial Garden.

a quiet place for relaxation and meditation. Students, faculty, and visitors take advantage of the garden to study and duplicate design styles.

Size
2½ acres

Features
This is a small garden, but great things can be found in small packages. Beautifully maintained, the entire landscape flows almost imperceptibly from one garden to the next as the pathways twist and turn, tempting the visitor to continue. The main features of this established garden are the Formal Boxwood Garden, two courtyards, the Terrace Garden, the Perennial Garden, and the Arboretum. There is also Hubert, a very friendly and very large domestic yellow cat who serves in an unofficial capacity as greeter, mouser, and general overseer.

Directions
From I-85, take Exit 53 (US 441/GA 15), travel south for 20 miles, and take the US 441 South/GA 10 Loop. Travel 6 miles, take the Watkinsville/Madison Exit (South Milledge Avenue), and travel north toward Athens. Travel 1.2 miles to South Lumpkin Street, turn right, and travel 1.4 miles. The garden is on the right. However, proceed another 0.1 mile to Broad Street and turn right to use public parking. There is parking behind the garden; it can

be accessed by turning right at Bocock Street (the street just before Broad Street). Be aware, however, that space during weekdays is limited. This parking area is recommended only for weekend or holiday visits.

Tips
Springtime is the best time for any garden, and this garden, with its spring planting of azaleas, flowering trees, and shrubs, is spectacular. However, special care has been taken to provide a broad spectrum of botanical colors throughout the seasons, so a visit at just about any time can be enjoyable. When traveling to this garden, it is important to remember that it is part of a very busy college campus. This creates parking problems, so it is wise to either visit on the weekend or arrive early during weekdays. If you wish to visit the Garden Club Museum, prior arrangements are advised even for weekday visits.

Accessibility
Designated parking is available, but most of the front garden is not accessible to the disabled.

Side Trips
The State Botanical Garden of Georgia (pages 18–23) and Sandy Creek Nature Center (pages 16–17), both in Athens, are less than 20 minutes from the garden. Vines Botanical Gardens (pages 81–85) is located 35 miles to the west in Loganville.

Sandy Creek Nature Center

Address
205 Old Commerce Road
Athens, Georgia 30607-1011
706-613-3615

Hours
The trails are open year-round from sunrise to sunset. The office, the science center, and Walker Discovery Hall are open Monday through Friday from 8:00 a.m. to 5:00 p.m. From March to mid-November, they are also open on Saturday from noon to 5:00 p.m.

Fees
There is no general admission charge. Nominal fees are charged for student groups.

History
Located in the environmentally diverse Piedmont of Georgia between Sandy Creek and the North Oconee River, Sandy Creek Nature Center was established in 1978 through a cooperative effort among the city of Athens, Clarke County, and local landowners for the pupose of heightening the environmental awareness of local citizens. As part of the Athens–Clarke County Department of Arts and Environmental Education, Sandy Creek Nature Center is an integral part of the county's greenway system. The greenways are managed, interconnected natural areas designed to consider man's needs in conjunction with the needs of natural systems and to arrive at an environmental balance beneficial to both. The nature center has developed an extensive community outreach program that offers a wide range of educational programs tailored to meet the needs of various community groups.

Size
225 acres

Features

The more than 4 miles of trails at the center—including Kingfisher Pond Trail, Oconee Trail, and Levee Trail—provide visitors access to habitats typical of the Georgia Piedmont. The habitats represented are upland woods, fields, and marshlands. The center's other features include the Interpretive Center, the Claypit Pond, brick factory ruins, and a cabin. Access to Cook's Trail, a 4.1-mile trail connecting Sandy Creek Nature Center with Sandy Creek Park, is located near the parking lot.

Directions

From I-85, take Exit 53 (US 441/GA 15) and travel south for 19.5 miles. The entrance to the center is on the right.

Tips

All trails are self-guided and well marked. Brochures which include trail maps are available at the center during office hours. Cook's Trail takes approximately two and a half to three hours to hike. If you are accessing Cook's Trail from Sandy Creek Nature Center, make sure you allow enough time to return to your vehicle, as the gates of the center close at 5:00 p.m. It is advisable to avoid some trails during periods of heavy rain, as certain areas are subject to flooding. Groups desiring programs tailored to a specific environmental interest can call the center in advance of their visit.

Accessibility

Designated parking and ramps allow access to the Interpretive Center. Paved roads allow vehicle access to some of the areas, but disabled persons may require assistance to access the nature trails.

Side Trips

Founders Memorial Garden (pages 10–15) and the State Botanical Garden of Georgia (pages 18–23), both in Athens, are less than a 20-minute drive from the nature center. Vines Botanical Gardens (pages 81–85) is located 35 miles west of Athens in Loganville.

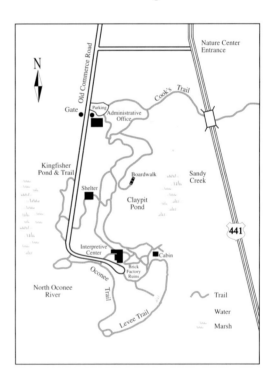

State Botanical Garden of Georgia

Address
2450 South Milledge Avenue
Athens, Georgia 30605-1624
706-542-1244

Hours
Open daily from 8:00 a.m. to sunset. The visitor center/conservatory complex is open Monday through Saturday from 9:00 a.m. to 4:30 p.m. and Sunday from 11:30 a.m. to 4:30 p.m. It is closed on major holidays.

Fees
None

History
The brainchild of Dr. Francis E. Johnstone, Jr., the State Botanical Garden of Georgia was proposed in December 1967 as a "living plant library" designed to benefit students and faculty in studies related to botany, horticulture, and landscape architecture. He avoided the term *botanical garden* in his proposal, since a botanical garden and arboretum had at one time existed on the campus. By 1907, both the garden and arboretum had fallen under the foot of expansion. Hoping to avoid a repeat of history, Johnstone approached the new garden from the perspective of its being an educational facility rather than just a "garden."

Johnstone's proposal was well received by the Campus Planning and Improvement Committee, university president Fred Davidson, and the Board of Regents. By 1969, the University of Georgia Botanical Garden, as it was originally

The Annual/Perennial Garden is one of the eleven display gardens at the State Botanical Garden of Georgia.

The visitor center/conservatory includes a ten-thousand-square-foot atrium which houses hundreds of plants.

called, was a reality. In 1984, the 293-acre garden was renamed the State Botanical Garden of Georgia in order to accurately reflect its role in developing and implementing statewide research and education programs in conjunction with various private and public organizations and agencies.

Supported by a number of Georgia horticultural organizations, the garden grew to its present size in 1990, when a twenty-acre tract of wetlands near the Middle Oconee River was obtained. That same year, the Board of Advisors recognized the importance of planned growth and appropriate land management and adopted a master plan.

Size

313 acres

Features

This garden, often referred to as a "living labo-ratory," has eleven different outdoor gardens, a conservatory, and a master plan which calls for an additional eight gardens and an arboretum. The Shade Garden, the Dunson Native Flora Garden, the Faust Dahlia Garden, the Turner Memorial Rose Garden, the Ballew Herb Gar-den, the Annual/Perennial Garden, the Rhodo-dendron Garden, the Ground Cover Collection, the Galle Native Azalea Garden, the Trial Garden, and the International Garden display a wide variety of plants which thrive in the mild Georgia climate. Other features include a chapel, nature trails, and the Callaway Building, which houses a library.

Indian pinks (Spigela marilandica) and other wildflowers native to Georgia can be found in the Dunson Native Flora Garden.

Directions

From I-85, take Exit 53 (US 441/GA 15), trav-el south for 20 miles, and take the US 441 South/GA 10 Loop. Travel 6 miles, take the Watkinsville/Madison Exit (South Milledge Avenue), and travel south. The garden is on the right after 1 mile.

Tips

There is so much to see in this sprawling garden that it's easy to get sidetracked by the beautiful plantings. In order not to miss anything, begin your tour at the visitor center/conservatory. Here, you can find out what's in bloom and pick up a map to help you maximize your visit. The wild-flowers begin blooming around the end of March. Blooming times for other plant species are outlined in a schedule available at the garden. For those who prefer wildlife to plant life, there are five miles of well-marked nature trails which provide excellent bird-watching opportunities.

Accessibility

The visitor center/conservatory is wheelchair accessible, and there are designated parking spaces for disabled persons. Most garden trails are paved for easy access, but access to the nature trails is limited.

Side Trips

Founders Memorial Garden (pages 10–15) and Sandy Creek Nature Center (pages 16–17), both in Athens, are located less than 20 minutes from the garden. Vines Botanical Gardens (pages 81–85) is located 35 miles to the west in Loganville.

A wide array of annuals and perennials
demonstrates what is available for the
home gardener's landscape.

Atlanta Botanical Garden

Address

Piedmont Park at the Prado
P.O. Box 77246
Atlanta, Georgia 30357-7246
404-876-5858 or 404-876-5859

Hours

Open Tuesday through Sunday from 9:00 a.m. to 6:00 p.m. October through March from and 9:00 a.m. to 7:00 p.m. April through September. Closed Monday except on holidays. The conservatory opens at 10:00 a.m. The garden is closed on Thanksgiving, Christmas Day, and New Year's Day.

The moon gate at the Japanese Garden frames a view of the Lanier Terrace.

Fees

Yes. Discounts are available for children, senior citizens, and students. Admission is waived on Thursday after 1:00 p.m.

History

Twenty years ago, Atlanta Botanical Garden was nothing more than an ambitious plan for an overgrown section of historic Piedmont Park. Since that time, it has blossomed into one of the South's finest botanical gardens, dedicated to developing and maintaining plant collections for display, education, research, conservation, and the enjoyment of the thousands of visitors it receives each year.

In 1977, a group of Atlanta citizens responded to the city's need for additional green space by establishing the garden on property leased from the city. Ann Crammond, the first executive director of the garden, four paid staff members, and a number of dedicated volunteers

nurtured the fledgling garden. Supporters and staff members recognized the need for a visitor center and other improvements, and fund-raising began in 1982. In one year's time, enough money was raised to build the visitor center. In 1988, the garden hosted the first Atlanta Flower Show. The following year, construction on the Dorothy Chapman Fuqua Conservatory was completed. Funded by a gift from J. B. Fuqua and named in honor of his wife—a garden volunteer

and trustee—the conservatory was designed by Heery Architects and Engineers of Atlanta. By 1993, the garden was operating community outreach programs, including a "plantmobile" program and a plant hotline (404-888-4769).

Wisteria and the sound of running water combine to enrich the garden experience.

The Dorothy Chapman Fuqua Conservatory, built
in 1989, contains twenty-three thousand square
feet of display area for a variety of plant species.

Non-hardy plant collections, some
rare, threatened, or endangered,
are featured in the conservatory.

Isobel, by Stern and Hougen, tiptoes through a garden near the Alston Overlook.

Throughout the year, programs designed to capture the interest of everyone from novice gardener to landscape architect are sponsored or hosted by Atlanta Botanical Garden. Today, the garden continues to be an integral part of the community, working toward educating the public on the importance of conservation.

Size
30 acres

Features
The array of gardens demonstrates creative uses of plants which flourish in the moderate Georgia climate. Specialty gardens include the Rose Garden, the Herb Garden, the Vegetable Garden, the Fragrance Garden, the Fern Garden, the Summer Bulb Garden, the Japanese Garden, the Rock Garden, and the Native Aquatic Plants Garden. Lining the pathways from one garden to another are collections of ornamental grasses, conifers, drought-tolerant plants, camellias, shrubs, vines, and much more. The most notable feature of the garden is the Dorothy Chapman Fuqua Conservatory, twenty-three thousand square feet of botanical paradise. The conservatory showcases many plant species, including orchids, carnivorous plants, and endangered plants. Right next door to the conservatory is the Desert House, where succulents from around the world are on display. A 1.25-mile hiking trail is across from the garden's main entrance in the Storza Woods, one of the few inner-city hardwood forests left in Atlanta. Additionally, the garden features a gift shop with a greenhouse and the Sheffield Botanical Library, where more than two thousand volumes are available for on-site research.

Directions
From I-85/75, take Exit 100 (North Street-US 78/278), travel east 0.5 mile, turn left onto Piedmont Avenue Northeast, and travel 1.5 miles. The garden entrance is on the right.

Tips
Atlanta's traffic problems are almost as famous as its baseball team and its restaurants, so be prepared. During weekends, holidays, and special events, parking at the garden is limited, so you may want to use public transportation. When visiting the Dorothy Chapman Fuqua Conservatory, enhance your visit by renting the thirty-minute audio tour, taped in five different languages.

Accessibility
Designated parking, ramps, and paved walkways allow extensive access to the garden and the conservatory for disabled persons.

Side Trips
There are four other gardens in the Atlanta area (see pages 32–43).

ATLANTA HISTORY CENTER

Address

130 West Paces Ferry Road, NW
Atlanta, Georgia   30305-1366
404-814-4000

Hours

Open Monday through Saturday from 10:00 a.m. to 5:30 p.m. and Sunday from noon to 5:30 p.m. Closed Thanksgiving, Christmas Eve, Christmas Day, and New Year's Day. The hours for Martin Luther King Day, Presidents' Day, Memorial Day, Independence Day, Labor Day, Columbus Day, Veterans Day, and New Year's Eve are noon to 5:30 p.m.

Fees

Yes. Discounts are available for students, senior citizens, and children. Group rates are available with advance reservations. There is an additional charge for historic house tours. Admission to the McElreath Hall Library and Archives is free.

History

In 1966, the Atlanta Historical Society embarked on a path of preservation with the acquisition of the Swan House, built in 1928, and ten acres of gardens. The Swan House and Garden became the cornerstone of a collection of nineteenth-century Georgia farm buildings, including a barn, a blacksmith shop, a separate kitchen, and a farmhouse. The house, built around 1845, was home to the Robert Smith family until 1967.

The society did not limit its collection activities to buildings. Over the years, it amassed a library of nearly 3.5 million items, including prints, photographs, books, drawings, public records, postcards, scrapbooks, and maps of Georgia and Atlanta. In 1975, McElreath Hall was completed to provide an appropriate place to house this growing collection. In 1993, the society opened the Atlanta History Museum. The museum houses traveling and permanent exhibits and the Museum Gift Shop. It also provides space for educational programs and administrative offices.

The Swan House, home of the Edward
Inman family during the 1920s, was
designed by Philip Trammel Shutze.

The Frank A. Smith Rhododendron
Garden features various plants that
flourish under shady conditions.

Size

33 acres

Features

It's hard to imagine, as you stroll around the Mary Howard Gilbert Memorial Quarry Garden enjoying the wildflowers, that you're in one of the largest cities in the country. As you move from the wildflowers up through Swan Woods Trail, you will find yourself in the middle of the magnificent landscape surrounding the Swan House. The Formal Boxwood Garden and the elegant expanse of lawn, complete with statues and fountain, tell the tale of the new Southern aristocracy. The rest of the center's landscape is dotted with gardens such as the Frank A. Smith Rhododendron Garden, the Cherry-Sims Asian-American Garden, and the Gardens for Peace, all of which celebrate the wide variety of plants that can be grown in the South. Other features at the center include the McElreath Hall Library and Archives, the Atlanta History Museum, the Swan House and Garden, the Tullie Smith House and Farm, the Museum Gift Shop, the Swan Coach House Restaurant, the Coca-Cola Cafe, and the Victorian Playhouse.

Directions

From I-75, take Exit 106 (Moores Mill Road), travel west 1.6 miles to West Paces Ferry Road, and turn right. Travel 1.1 miles and turn right onto Slaton Drive. The entrance is on the right after 0.1 mile.

Tips

Ticket sales for the garden continue until 4:30 p.m., but you should allow at least three hours to tour the center. Maps are available in English, Japanese, French, Spanish, and German. During the year, the center hosts a variety of lectures, festivals, and other special events. A program calendar is available by calling the center. The cafe has counter service Monday through Saturday from 11:00 a.m. to 5:00 p.m.; the restaurant is open for lunch Monday through Saturday from 11:30 a.m. to 2:30 p.m.; and the Museum Gift Shop is open Monday through Saturday from 10:00 a.m. to 5:00 p.m. and Sunday from noon to 5:00 p.m. The McElreath Hall Library and Archives is closed on Sunday.

Accessibility

The Atlanta History Museum and McElreath Hall are accessible to disabled persons. Designated parking is available. Paved pathways provide easy access to different parts of the gardens. Large-print reading materials are available for the various exhibitions.

Side Trips

There are four other gardens in the Atlanta area (see pages 25–31 and 38–43).

Statues and fountains accent the gardens around the Swan House.

CATOR WOOLFORD GARDENS

Address
1815 Ponce de Leon Avenue, NW
Atlanta, Georgia 30307-1323
404-377-3836

Hours
Open daily from sunrise to sunset

Fees
None

History
Cator Woolford Gardens is located on what was once Jacqueland, Woolford's thirty-three-acre estate named for the French orphan he and his wife supported. In 1921, Woolford, president and founder of the Retail Credit Company, engaged Philadelphia landscape architect Richard B. Cridland to design the gardens in historic Druid Hills, a suburb of Atlanta designed by Frederick Law Olmsted in 1893. In 1949, the estate was purchased and placed in trust by the Childrens Rehabilitation Center.

Size
6 acres

Features
Designed to provide therapeutic gardening and nature experiences for disabled individuals, Cator Woolford Gardens features the Perennial Garden, the Bog Garden, the Wildflower Glen, the Rock Garden, and a virgin forest. Mature native rhododendron, azaleas, and hollies line the woodland trail, which is accented with dogwoods and the soothing sounds of a stream. The garden structures are original to the Woolford estate.

Directions
From I-85/75, take Exit 100 (North Street-US 78/278) and travel east 0.5 mile. Turn left onto Piedmont Avenue Northeast, then right at the next light onto Ponce de Leon Avenue Northeast (US 29/78/278-GA 8). Travel 3 miles to Clifton Road Northeast. Turn right at the light, make an immediate left onto South Ponce de Leon Avenue Northeast, and travel 0.2 mile. The entrance is on the right.

Cator Woolford often used the gardens for entertaining friends and business associates.

Tips

If you are familiar with these lovely gardens and haven't visited in a while, go back. The gardens and buildings have been extensively renovated. As always, spring is the ideal time to view any garden, and this one is surely no exception. However, considering the variety of plant materials in the landscape, every season holds great promise.

Accessibility

The gardens and buildings are fully accessible to disabled persons.

Side Trips

There are four other gardens in the Atlanta area (see pages 25–37 and 40–43).

FERNBANK SCIENCE CENTER

Address
156 Heaton Park Drive, NE
Atlanta, Georgia 30307-1398
404-378-4311

Hours
Open Monday from 8:30 a.m. to 5:00 p.m., Tuesday through Friday from 8:30 a.m. to 10:00 p.m., Saturday from 10:00 a.m. to 5:00 p.m., and Sunday from 1:00 p.m. to 5:00 p.m.

Fees
No admission is charged to the center or to Fernbank Forest, but there is a charge for planetarium shows.

History
Fernbank Science Center, part of the Department of Instruction of the DeKalb County schools, began operation in 1967 after several years of planning by the Fernbank Board of Trustees and the DeKalb County Board of Education. Designed to supplement the education of area students, the center has utilized interpretive and innovative scientific programs to excite and enlighten more than fifteen million visitors. The center is part of the Fernbank complex, which also includes the Fernbank Museum of Natural History and Fernbank Forest.

Size
65 acres

Features
The entryway to the center showcases a formal arrangement of seasonal plants in attractive brick planters. At the rear of the center is Fernbank Forest. Its two miles of paved trails move past mature hardwoods, wildflowers, a pond, and instructional shelters. A section of trail has been outfitted with guide ropes to aid the visually impaired. Taped narration and Braille recorders are available at the center. The

primeval Fernbank Forest offers other features such as an underground window, the Horticultural Garden, a greenhouse, the Harrison Cistern, Elephant Rock, and Hodgson House, which serves as a preparation laboratory. The center offers natural history exhibits, agricultural demonstrations, and one of the nation's largest planetariums.

Directions

From I-85, take Exit 100 (North Street-US 78/278), travel east for 0.5 mile, turn left onto Piedmont Avenue Northeast, then right at the next light onto Ponce de Leon Avenue Northeast (US 29/78/278-GA 8). Travel 4 miles to Artwood Road and turn left. Travel 0.3 mile and turn right onto Heaton Park Drive. The science center is on the left across from an elementary school after 0.2 mile.

Tips

Most visitors are school groups on scheduled tours of the forest on weekdays from 8:30 a.m. to 5:00 p.m. The general public can visit the forest weekdays from 2:00 p.m. until 5:00 p.m. Please note that forest inhabitants include the poisonous copperhead snake, which occasionally warms itself on the trails.

Accessibility

Designated parking, ramps, and paved pathways allow easy access for disabled persons.

Side Trips

There are four other gardens in the Atlanta area (see pages 25–39 and 42–43).

Mayapples (Podophyllum peltatum) are at home on the damp, shady floor of Fernbank Forest.

ROBERT L. STATON ROSE GARDEN

Address
156 Heaton Park Drive, NE
Atlanta, Georgia 30307-1221
404-378-4311

Hours
Open daily from sunrise to sunset

Fees
None

History

As a teenager, Robert Staton had a rose garden in a corner of his mother's vegetable garden, where both he and she could enjoy the blooms. Today, his rose garden is on the grounds of the Fernbank Museum of Natural History for everyone who loves roses to enjoy.

While still in his teens, Robert joined the American Rose Society (ARS). In 1983, while working for Fernbank Science Center, he devel-oped a proposal for the garden that now bears his name. The garden was named in his memory after his death in December 1990.

Size
1 acre

Features
More than 1,300 roses representing at least 250 varieties of miniature roses, hybrid tea roses, and climbing roses are planted in this sunny garden. Many have the distinction of being past winners of the All-American Rose Selections (AARS). In the beds of miniature roses, you will find past winners of the ARS's Award of Excellence. You may also find unnamed roses identified with a series of numbers. These roses are currently entered in a rose trial and are evaluated periodically to determine if they are suitable for the home landscape.

Directions

From I-85/75, take Exit 100 (North Street-US 78/278), travel east 0.5 mile, turn left onto Piedmont Avenue Northeast, then right at the next light onto Ponce de Leon Avenue Northeast (US 29/78/278-GA 8). Travel 3 miles to Clifton Road and turn left at the light. At 0.2 mile, turn right into the entrance of the Fernbank Museum of Natural History at 767 Clifton Road. Parking for the rose garden is on either side of the building on the right.

Tips

Roses in the Atlanta area begin blooming around the middle of May, depending upon the spring weather, and bloom until frost. As a test garden for the AARS and the ARS, this is an excellent garden from which to get ideas for the roses which will do well in the local climate. If you would like additional information regarding the rose garden, address inquiries to Fernbank Science Center (see pages 40–41).

Accessibility

Designated parking is available, and ramps allow access to the garden. There are some sidewalks, but the grassy pathways between the rose beds may necessitate assistance for some disabled persons.

Side Trips

There are four other gardens in the Atlanta area (see pages 25–41).

Bonica, a shrub rose introduced in 1985, was an All-American Rose Selections winner for 1987.

OLD GOVERNMENT HOUSE

Address

432 Telfair Street

Augusta, Georgia 30901-2452

706-821-1812

Hours

Open daily from sunrise to sunset. The house is open Monday through Friday from 9:00 a.m. to 5:00 p.m.

Fees

None

History

Built in 1801 in the Federal style, the Old Government House was originally used as the municipal building for the city of Augusta and the county of Richmond. Later, when the structure was used as a residence, additions were made which modified its architecture to reflect the Regency and Greek Revival styles. Eventually, the structure fell into disrepair. But fortunately, Augustans realized the value of preserving their history and began a restoration in the mid-1980s. Work was completed in 1989.

Size

¼ acre

Features

This small front-yard garden reflects Augusta's love affair with the colorful azalea. Other features include dogwood trees, crape myrtle, magnolias, camellias, seasonal plantings, and a ginkgo tree said to have been planted when President George Washington visited the area in the late 1700s.

Directions

From I-20, take Exit 66 (Riverwalk Parkway/GA 104) and travel east on GA 104 for 4.7 miles to Thirteenth Street. Turn left onto Thirteenth Street, turn right onto Reynolds Street, and travel 0.6 mile to Eighth Street. Turn right, travel 0.3 mile to Telfair Street, and turn left. The Old Government House is on the right at 0.5 mile.

Tips

The Old Government House features changing art exhibits, so call for information. Augusta,

home of the Master's Golf Tournament, held in early April, is clothed in a variety of horticultural colors as the azaleas burst onto the scene the first of the month.

Accessibility

Designated parking for disabled persons is available at the rear of the house. Ramps allow access to the building. Paved sidewalks allow access to the garden.

Side Trips

Also in Augusta are Pendleton King Park (pages 46–47) and Riverwalk (pages 48–51). Both are a short drive from the Old Government House.

PENDLETON KING PARK

Address

Tree and Landscape Department
1568 Broad Street
Augusta, Georgia 30901-1358
706-722-5891

Hours

Open Monday through Saturday from 8:00 a.m. to 8:00 p.m. and Sunday from 8:00 a.m. to 6:00 p.m.

Fees

None

History

Born in 1799, John Pendleton King moved to Augusta from Kentucky and began a business career which included becoming president of the Georgia Railroad and Banking Company. His daughter, Louise King, was instrumental in enacting legislation which led to the organization of the Georgia Society for the Prevention of Cruelty to Animals. Their kinsman Henry B. King made provisions in his will that helped to establish Augusta's largest inner-city park.

Size

64 acres

Features

Pendleton King Park offers an eighteen-station disk golf course played with a Frisbee instead of a ball. Other recreational facilities include tennis courts, a fitness court, and a playground. Picnic shelters, gazebos, and benches encourage visitors to take their time and feed the ducks. Botanical features at the park include the Walter A. Wilson Camellia Garden, the Sunken Blue Garden, the Augusta Arboretum, and lots of azaleas. Children will enjoy the playground and delight in the United States Army tank on display.

Directions

From I-20, take Exit 66 (Riverwalk Parkway/GA 104 East), travel 4.7 miles to Thirteenth Street (GA 4 South), and turn right. Follow GA 4 South through town for 3.1 miles (watch for signs) to Milledgeville Road and turn right. Travel 0.6 mile to Kissingbower Road and turn right. The park is on the right at 1.1 miles.

Tips

The abundant azaleas in the park are at their peak during the first part of April. The arboretum located on the grounds was developed within the past five years and will continue to expand as the park is improved.

The Sunken Blue Garden surrounds the visitor with azaleas, peace, and quiet.

Accessibility

Designated parking, ramps, sidewalks, and paved pathways through the arboretum and park provide easy access for disabled persons.

Side Trips

Also in Augusta are the Old Government House (pages 44–45) and Riverwalk (pages 48–51). Both are a short drive from the park.

RIVERWALK

Address
Augusta/Richmond County Convention
  and Visitors Bureau
P.O. Box 1331
Augusta, Georgia 30903-1331
706-823-6600

Hours
Open daily from sunrise to sunset

Fees
None

History
General James Oglethorpe, founding father of the city of Savannah in 1733, moved up the Savannah River in 1736 and founded the city of Augusta. The river figured prominently in Augusta's success as its link to commercial growth. It was also an unpredictable menace capable of washing away settlers and their dreams. In the early 1900s, community leaders reined in the river by building a levee.

During the mid-1980s, Augusta's leaders recognized the potential impact the Savannah River could have on downtown revitalization efforts and made plans to utilize the levee. They soon discovered it would take an act of Congress to use the levee for anything other than a protective barrier. Finally, in 1987, the $16 million Riverwalk was officially begun.

Size
5 city blocks along the Savannah River

Features
This unique attraction allows visitors to stroll beside the banks of the Savannah River on two beautifully landscaped promenades. One, built at the top of the levee, affords an incredible view of different areas of the city and the river. The second promenade, just below the first, winds above the bank for an up-close view of the river. Along the five blocks are azaleas, dogwoods, river birch trees, and seasonal plantings. Other features include the Japanese Garden, a

gift from the people of Japan, and the Celtic Cross, which marks the site of Fort Augusta, built by General Oglethorpe in 1736. There are also a playground for the children, picnic tables, benches, and a full-service marina and dock with access to riverboat tours.

Augusta lives up to its nickname, the "Garden City," each spring when thousands of azaleas bloom.

Directions

From I-20, take Exit 66 (Riverwalk Parkway/GA 104) and travel east on GA 104 for 4.7 miles to Thirteenth Street. Turn left onto Thirteenth Street and then take the first right, which is Reynolds Street. Travel 0.8 mile to Riverwalk and turn left at Sixth Street for public parking.

Tips

Riverwalk, located along the Savannah River, is the site of many of Augusta's special events. If you would like to plan your visit in conjunction with any of these events, call the Riverwalk Special Events Office at 706-821-1754. A visit to Augusta in the spring is recommended. Spring is itself a special event here, as hundreds of thousands of azaleas and thousands of dogwoods bloom throughout the city. When planning a spring visit, make reservations early, as lodgings are usually booked for the Master's Golf Tournament, held the first full week in April.

Accessibility

Paved pathways and ramps give disabled individuals broad access to the Riverwalk area.

Side Trips

The Old Government House (pages 44–45) is located only a few miles from Riverwalk, as is Pendleton King Park (pages 46–47).

The Savannah River, Augusta's first highway, brought settlers and prosperity to the city.

ANTIQUE ROSE EMPORIUM

Address
Route 10, Box 2220
Dahlonega, Georgia 30533-9801
706-864-5884

Hours
Open Tuesday through Saturday from 10:00 a.m. to
5:30 p.m. and Sunday from 12:30 p.m. to 5:30 p.m.
Closed Monday, New Year's Day, Easter, Fourth of
July, Thanksgiving, and Christmas.

Fees
None

History
Dahlonega, site in 1828 of America's first
significant gold rush, now has another precious commodity in its soil–Old Garden Roses.
The Antique Rose Emporium, whose roots are
in the small Texas town of Independence,
branched into Georgia in 1993. The Texas location opened in 1984 and championed the come-
back of the low-maintenance Old Garden Rose
as an important part of the Southern landscape.

Size
2 acres

Features
Old Garden Roses, companion perennials, and
indigenous species are used in the Display
Garden to reflect the Southern botanical heritage. Other botanical features include herbs,
annuals, and shrubs which thrive in the long
summers and mild winters. Formal and informal design features have been used in the
Display Garden, whose focal point, the
Jackson-Ridley House, is accented by a picket
fence. In the area around the house are the
Formal Perennial Border, the Knot Garden, the
Walled Garden, a rose-covered walkway, and
the Polyantha Bed.

Directions

From I-285, take Exit 19 (US 19/GA 400) and travel north on the Turner McDonald Parkway for 46 miles to where GA 400 ends at GA 60. Cross GA 60 and continue straight on Long Branch Road for 6.5 miles, at which point Long Branch Road becomes Copper Mines Road. Continue on Copper Mines Road for 2 miles to Cavender's Creek Road and turn right. The entrance is on the left at 0.5 mile.

Tips

More than roses can be found at the emporium, so call for blooming information. If you have what's left of Grandmother's rosebush in your yard and would like to have it identified, this is the place to start. Remember, it will be easier to identify if flower, foliage, and stem are kept fresh.

Rose de Rescht, a very fragrant damask rose, is one of the many varieties of Old Garden Roses regaining popularity.

Accessibility

The gift shop and the Display Garden are accessible to disabled persons. Gravel pathways and moderate inclines in some areas will necessitate assistance.

Side Trips

Fifty miles north in Hiawassee is the Fred Hamilton Rhododendron Garden (pages 72–77). Thirty miles southeast in Gainesville is Elachee Nature Science Center (pages 68–69).

DeKalb College Botanical Gardens

Address
3251 Panthersville Road
Decatur, Georgia 30034-3832
404-244-5052

Hours
Open daily from sunrise to sunset

Fees
None

History
In the spring of 1990, students at DeKalb College started this garden, which soon became known as the Wildflower Center of Georgia. Dedicated to the preservation and propagation of indigenous plant species, it is Georgia's largest all-native garden. Eventually, the garden will showcase more than two thousand plant species. Jointly administered by DeKalb College and DeKalb County, it is a classroom for students and others interested in horticulture.

Size
4 acres

Features
Situated in a flood plain, the garden features wildflowers and other indigenous species planted near a creek and along a woodland nature trail. More than twelve hundred species of plants are represented, some of which are considered rare or endangered. The gardens' specialty is rare, hard-to-find, hard-to-grow native plants. A collection of ferns and the colorful Perennial Garden are also featured. Specimen plants ideal for Georgia's landscape are displayed throughout the grounds.

Directions
From I-285, take Exit 36 (GA 155/Flat Shoals Parkway), follow the parkway for 0.5 mile to Clifton Springs Road, and turn right. Travel 0.7 mile to Panthersville Road, turn left, and proceed another 0.2 mile. The parking area for the gardens is on the right.

Smooth Solomon's-seal
(Polygonatum biflorum) is
at home along a creek bank.

Tips

In the middle of April and again in mid-July, these gardens put on a spectacular show. However, during heavy rains, the gardens are subject to flooding. A weekend visit is recommended in order to avoid the parking difficulties inherent to college campuses. Four plant sales—two in the spring and two in the fall—are the main source of funding for the gardens.

Accessibility

Access for disabled persons is limited.

Side Trips

There are five gardens in the Atlanta area (see pages 25–43).

Dunwoody Nature Center

Address
5343 Roberts Drive
Dunwoody, Georgia 30338-3834
770-394-3322

Hours
Open daily from sunrise to sunset. The building
is open by appointment Monday through Friday,
usually from 9:00 a.m. to 5:00 p.m.

Fees
None

History

Established for the purpose of developing,
improving, and preserving Dunwoody Park,
part of the DeKalb County Parks and Recreation Department, Dunwoody Nature Center
is a wonderful natural classroom which offers a
variety of environmental programs throughout
the year. Relatively new, the nature center
began as a volunteer project supported by local
citizens. These citizens were keenly interested in
habitat preservation and in educating future
generations to the importance of the environment and the responsible conservation and
management of resources.

In the beginning, only forty-one members
volunteered to participate in the project, which
sought to improve not only the grounds but the
park building as well. These members also worked hard to develop a community outreach program which would swell the volunteer ranks
and bring to light the importance of public
green spaces.

Today, the center is actively supported by
more than two hundred members. This has
allowed it to increase the number of programs
offered to the public each year from forty-eight

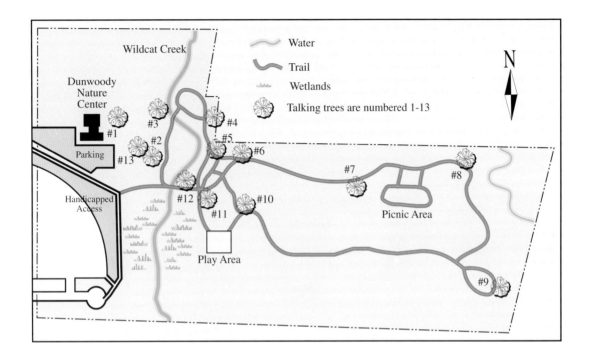

Wildcat Creek

Dunwoody
Nature
Center

#3

#1

Parking

#2

#13

Handicapped
Access

#12

#11

Play Area

Water

Trail

Wetlands

Talking trees are numbered 1-13

N

#4

#5

#6

#10

#7

#8

Picnic Area

#9

to more than three hundred. Active member-
ship has also allowed the center to broaden the
scope of its educational programming, which
appeals not only to preschoolers and school-age
children but to adults as well.

The future of the center appears to be
bright, thanks to the implementation of a five-
year strategic operations plan and the development of a master plan designed to improve
natural resource protection and expand the
present facility.

Size

12 acres

Features

A major highlight, especially for children and
interested adults, is the thirteen talking trees
strategically placed along the park trail. The
trail makes a 1.3-mile loop, taking the visitor on
a scenic trip through the various habitats found
at the center: a wetland, a Piedmont creek, a

hardwood and pine forest, and a meadow. Children will appreciate the well-equipped play area. The myriad programs offered throughout the year include the Garden Tour, held in May on the weekend after Mother's Day; the Butterfly Festival, held the last Saturday in July; and the Bats and Bones Halloween Animal Encounter, held in October.

Directions

From I-285, take Exit 19 (US 19/GA 400), travel north on the Turner McDonald Parkway, and take Exit 6 (Northridge Road). Stay in the far left lane of the exit ramp and keep straight at the stop sign; you will be on Roberts Drive. Travel 2 miles to the entrance to the nature center, on the left at 5343 Roberts Drive.

A turtlehead bloom (Chelone glabra) peeks out above the leaflets.

Tips

You may want to visit the center during one of its many special events. Depending upon your area of interest, the center may have a program just for you. Most of the programs are geared toward children, but the center does offer family events and a gardening lecture series for adults. Write or call for a program guide, making sure to indicate your area of interest. Pets are welcome but must be kept on a leash. Picnic facilities are available on the grounds.

Accessibility

Designated parking and restroom facilities are available. A trail designed especially for disabled persons is scheduled to open in 1997. You may wish to call for a progress report.

Side Trips

Chattahoochee Nature Center (pages 122–23) is less than 10 miles northwest in Roswell. Dunwoody, located just north of Atlanta, is close to all of that city's gardens and nature centers (see pages 25–43).

COCHRAN MILL NATURE CENTER AND ARBORETUM

Address
P. O. Box 911
Fairburn, Georgia 30213-0911
770-306-0914

Hours
Open Monday through Saturday from 9:00 a.m. to 5:00 p.m. Open Sunday from 1:00 p.m. to 5:00 p.m., March through October. Closed most major holidays.

Fees
Yes

History
This privately owned nature center and arboretum, dedicated to educating the public about mankind's environmental responsibility to the earth and its inhabitants, was opened to the public in 1994. The center carries the name of the old gristmill built by Cheadle Cochran in the early 1800s. Cochran, a prosperous miller and farmer, was also a state senator who worked for legislation that established mail routes in Georgia. Today, due to the burning of the mill and dynamiting of the dam by vandals, very little of the old structure remains.

Size
50 acres

Features
Its proximity to the eight-hundred-acre county-owned Cochran Mill Park allows the center to share features such as hiking trails, native flora and fauna, and mill ruins. Other features include waterfalls, a low-element and a high-elements ropes challenge courses, and a wide variety of environmental programs. Throughout the year, special events such as the Father's Day Fishing Derby, the Halloween Hayride, and the Wild Trail Trot are held at the center.

Late-afternoon sun brightens the distinctively shaped leaves of a maple tree.

Directions

From I-85, take Exit 16 (Old National Highway/Roosevelt Highway) and follow the signs to South Fulton Parkway (Spur 14). Follow South Fulton Parkway for 15 miles until it ends. Turn right onto Rivertown Road, travel 2 miles to Cochran Mill Road, and turn left. The nature center is on the left at 0.2 mile.

Tips

This center has an extensive community outreach program designed to attract and educate nature lovers of all ages. Call or write for a program schedule. The environmental programs are offered on a first-come, first-served basis and are tailored to meet group needs. The Challenge-By-Choice courses, designed to enhance personal understanding and develop effective life skills, are available for business groups, sports teams, at-risk youths, and the physically challenged.

Accessibility

Designated parking is available. The center's building is accessible to disabled persons.

Side Trips

Twenty miles to the east is the William H. Reynolds Nature Preserve (pages 104–5) in Morrow. Thirty miles to the southeast is the Melvin L. Newman Wetlands Center (pages 70–71) in Hampton.

The unusual use of old millstones
adds another creative touch to
Massee Lane Gardens.

MASSEE LANE GARDENS, HOME OF THE AMERICAN CAMELLIA SOCIETY

Address

One Massee Lane
Fort Valley, Georgia 31030-9100
912-967-2358 or 912-967-2772

Hours

From December through March, the gardens are open Monday through Saturday from 9:00 a.m. to 5:00 p.m. and Sunday from 1:00 p.m. to 5:00 p.m. From April through November, they are open Monday through Friday from 9:00 a.m. to 4:00 p.m. The gardens are closed on most major holidays.

Fees

Yes. American Camellia Society members and children under twelve are admitted free.

History

Nestled beneath towering pines and surrounded by peach orchards and pecan groves as far as the eye can see, Massee Lane Gardens, home of the American Camellia Society, is a wonderland of beautiful blooms. The gardens are located on what was once an expansive antebellum plantation owned by Needham Massee. Massee, originally from North Carolina, acquired the plantation through a land lottery held in 1827 after the Creek Indians were moved west by government decree.

A small part of the plantation, still owned by descendants of Needham Massee, was purchased in the early 1900s by Dave Strother and his business partner, Dr. McArthur, in order to establish a peach-packing business. In 1936, the men experienced severe losses when the area was hit

by a powerful and destructive windstorm. Strother and McArthur's peach crop and most of the packing facility were destroyed.

Another casualty of the storm was a large pecan tree which occupied a place of honor in front of the overseer's house. Strother replaced it with a camellia japonica variety named Elegans. The plant promptly died, but Strother's love affair with the camellia began to take root. He liked the plant so much that he planted other camellias around the property.

Strother soon discovered he was not alone in his appreciation of this glorious flower. In 1945, he and other camellia enthusiasts founded the American Camellia Society. The society steadily grew as the camellia's popularity as a landscape staple began to sweep across the Southeast.

In the short span of twenty years, and after outgrowing two progressively larger facilities, the society was desperately in need of space to

The Abendroth Japanese Garden is one of several specialty gardens at Massee Lane Gardens.

Camellias, noted for their
vibrant and varied colors,
are not fragrant.

accommodate its growing ranks. Dave Strother, ever faithful to the society and desiring to preserve the beauty of his gardens for the future, donated his gardens and farm to the American Camellia Society. Once the exclusive domain of peach and pecan trees, the farmland slated to become a business sucess for Strother and McArthur became a mecca for camellia lovers everywhere.

Size
10 acres

Features
Camellias are the star of these charming, well-planted gardens, but the garden visitor will also discover such delightful specialty gardens as the Abendroth Japanese Garden, the Scheibert Rose Garden, the Formal Garden, the Awards Garden, and the Entry Garden. If horticultural history is your forte, the American Camellia Society Headquarters Library, which contains the world's largest collection of books on camellias, is available for research. Other attractions include a landscaped camellia greenhouse, a gift shop, the Mildred Stevens Taylor Gallery, and the Annabelle Lundy Fetterman Educational Museum. Together, the gallery and museum house the world's most extensive collection of Edward Marshall Boehm porcelains, along with works from other artists like Boleslaw Cybis, Susan Dorothy Doughty, and Sister Maria Innocentia Hummel.

Directions
From I-75, take Exit 46 (the Byron/Fort Valley Exit, GA 49), travel south 16.4 miles, and turn left onto Massee Lane. The gardens are on the right at 0.2 mile.

Tips
Camellias bloom from November through March, with the peak around the first part of February. Even though Fort Valley is located in central Georgia, be sure to bring more than just a sweater, as days during the camellia blooming season can be quite chilly. During the first part of February, the headquarters hosts the nine-day Camellia Festival, featuring activities designed to entertain and educate garden visitors. A variety of other plants, including roses, bulbs, flowering trees, and azaleas, dots the landscape of the beautifully maintained gardens. All visitors should start their tour with the fifteen-minute slide presentation.

Accessibility
Designated parking, ramps, and level ground make the gardens accessible to disabled persons. Wheelchairs are available for garden visitors.

Side Trips
Lockerly Arboretum (pages 98–103) is located 60 miles northeast, just outside Milledgeville. Callaway Gardens (pages 113–21), located in Pine Mountain, is 90 miles west.

ELACHEE NATURE SCIENCE CENTER

Address

2125 Elachee Drive
Gainesville, Georgia 30504-7158
770-535-1976

Hours

The trails are open daily from 8:00 a.m. to sunset. The nature center and museum are open Monday through Saturday from 10:00 a.m. to 5:00 p.m. The center is closed on Sunday, Thanksgiving, Christmas Eve, and Christmas.

Fees

Yes, for the nature center and museum. Discounts are available for children and center members. No fees are charged to use the nature trails.

History

Nestled in the Chicopee Woods Nature Preserve is Elachee Nature Science Center, whose name in Cherokee means "new green earth." The center and surrounding preserve represent the lion's share of a twenty-five-hundred-acre donation made in 1980 to the city of Gainesville and Hall County by the Chicopee Manufacturing Company. The donation came with the condition that it be used for recreational and educational facilities. The property, administered by the Chicopee Woods Area Park Commission, was divided into three sections and developed in keeping with the wishes of the donor. The Chicopee Agricultural Center was developed on one of the other sections, as was the Chicopee Woods Golf Course.

Size

1,200 acres

Features

Emphasis is placed on educating the public about the importance of nature. The center houses exhibits, classrooms, and a gift shop. It has three walking trails which vary in length and difficulty, Boulevard Trail being the easiest and shortest. Ed Dodd Trail and Boulevard Trail start at the center, and Mathis Trail branches off Ed Dodd Trail. Ed Dodd Trail and Mathis Trail are approximately 1 mile each. Other features of the center include the Wildlife Garden and Trail and museum tours.

Directions

From I-985, take Exit 4 (the Oakwood Exit) and follow GA 53 East for 0.4 mile. Turn left (north) onto GA 13 and travel 2.4 miles. The entrance to the nature center is on the right.

Tips

Although you can't access the entire twelve hundred acres, there is plenty to see from the trails, so bring binoculars and your bird and wildflower guides. Boulevard Trail is the best trail for small children and older adults. All trails are well marked. If you plan to be on the trails after the gate is locked at 5:00 p.m., be sure to park outside the gate. If you schedule your visit on the second Saturday of the month, you'll be in for a real treat. The center's naturalist and local experts pull out all the stops for the Second Saturdays Family Festivals. These events are free with museum admission and run from 11:00 a.m. to 2:00 p.m.

Accessibility

Designated parking is available, and the center's buildings are accessible to disabled persons. A trail designed for the disabled is in the works. Call the center for progress updates.

Side Trips

Thirty miles northwest are Dahlonega and the Antique Rose Emporium (pages 52–53). Thirty-five miles southeast are Athens and the State Botanical Garden of Georgia (pages 18–23), Founders Memorial Garden (pages 10–15), and Sandy Creek Nature Center (pages 16–17).

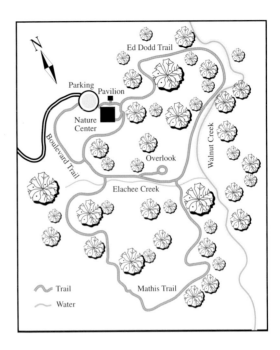

MELVIN L. NEWMAN WETLANDS CENTER

Address
2755 Freeman Road
Hampton, Georgia 30228-1684
770-603-5606

Hours
Open Wednesday through Sunday from 8:30 a.m. to 5:00 p.m.

Fees
None

History
Opened in 1995 and administered by the Clayton County Water Authority, the Melvin L. Newman Wetlands Center beautifully demonstrates the importance of preserving the precious wetland environment and conserving other valuable natural resources. Melvin L. Newman is a native of Oklahoma and general manager for the Clayton County Water Authority. The center named in his honor stands as a testament to the water authority's commitment to resource management. Newman, who began his career with the water authority as a draftsman in 1963, became general manager in 1983. Nationally recognized as a leader in his field, Newman is an avid conservationist who has implemented innovative programs geared toward utilizing treated wastewater and preserving the natural water supply.

Size
32 acres

Features
The wetland area is the main attraction. It is accessed via the 0.6-mile Wetland Trail. Along the trail are benches, covered areas, and a water fountain. The center includes a building complex which offers a variety of exhibits. Plans are in the works for a more extensive trail system. These trails will be for guided walks only. Call for progress reports.

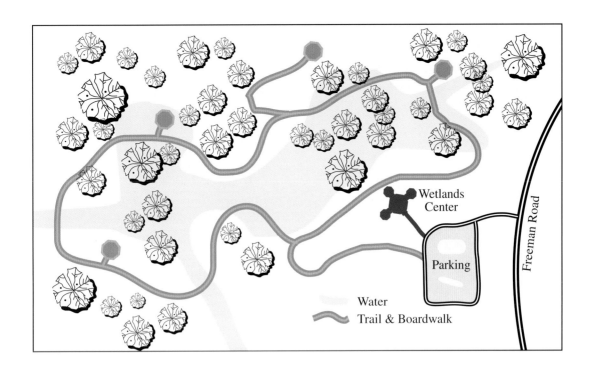

Water
Trail & Boardwalk

Directions

From I-75, take Exit 71 (McDonough Road), travel west toward Lovejoy for 6.2 miles, and turn right onto Freeman Road. The center is on the right at 1.4 miles.

Tips

More than two hundred species of birds migrate through the area, so bring your binoculars. You may want to bring along mosquito repellent during the summer months.

Accessibility

Designated parking is available. The entire center, including the trail, is accessible to disabled persons.

Side Trips

Located in Morrow, 23 miles north, is the William H. Reynolds Nature Preserve (pages 104–5). Located 26 miles to the northeast in Stockbridge is Panola Mountain State Conservation Park (pages 158–59).

FRED HAMILTON RHODODENDRON GARDEN

Address

P.O. Box 444
Hiawassee, Georgia 30546-0444
706-896-4191

Hours

Open daily from sunrise to sunset

Fees

None

History

Fred and Hazel Hamilton began their love affair with rhododendron in 1952 when they bought their first home in Atlanta. Their property was dotted with native azaleas and rhododendron. Later, when the Hamiltons moved to Towns County in northern Georgia, their interest broadened to include native wildflowers.

Over the next thirty years, they planted hybrid varieties of rhododendron, bringing their collection to nearly fifteen hundred plants.

They wanted to share the beauty of this native flower, which blooms from spring into early fall. Neighbors would visit the garden, but Fred Hamilton knew that more people would be able to appreciate it if it were in a more accessible location. In 1982, the Hamiltons donated their garden to the Georgia Mountain State Fair. An appropriate site was selected near Lake Chatuge within sight of Brasstown Bald, the highest point in Georgia, and more than fifteen hundred plants were moved the three miles to the new location. Since that time, more plants have been donated by the Hamiltons or added by the Georgia Mountain State Fair, expanding the collection to nearly two thousand plants representing more than four hundred varieties. In 1990, the first annual Rhododendron Festival was held in the garden.

Species such as flame azalea
(Rhododendron calendulaceum)
can be seen at the garden.

Size

17 acres

Features

Though this is the largest public rhododendron garden in Georgia, it has much more to offer the garden visitor: native azaleas, dogwood trees, tulip magnolias, lady-slippers, trilliums, and many other native wildflowers. Another feature of the garden is the trail which meanders within view of Lake Chatuge. The Fred Hamilton Rhododendron Garden is the site of the annual Rhododendron Festival, sponsored by the Hiawassee Area Chamber of Commerce. Adjacent to the garden is the Georgia Mountain State Fairgrounds, which sponsors special events during the year. The fairgrounds has a boat ramp for those who enjoy fishing, boating, or other water-related activities.

The iridescent color of rhododendron is just one of the reasons it's a Southern landscape favorite (previous page).

Directions

From Hiawassee, take US 76 West for 1 mile. The entrance to the garden and fairgrounds is on the right.

Tips

Peak season for the garden is a four- to six-week period usually beginning around the last week in April. At that time, the azaleas and the dogwood trees begin to bloom, followed by the first flush of rhododendron. Blooming in turn are trilliums, lady-slippers, other wildflower species, and tulip magnolias. The Georgia Mountain State Fairgrounds is a popular place, as is Lake Chatuge. If you are planning a visit to the garden, you may want to write or call the Georgia Mountain State Fair to obtain a schedule of events.

Accessibility

The well-maintained trails are bark-covered, which may decrease their accessibility for some disabled persons. Wheelchairs and walkers are difficult to maneuver on the trails.

Side Trips

Dahlonega, home of the Antique Rose Emporium (pages 52–53), is about 45 miles southwest. Located in Gainesville, 60 miles to the south, is Elachee Nature Science Center (pages 68–69).

Azalea varieties and dogwood
trees complement the abundant
plantings of rhododendron.

DAUSET TRAILS NATURE CENTER

Address

360 Mount Vernon Church Road
Jackson, Georgia 30233-4404
770-775-6798

Hours

Open Monday through Saturday from 9:00 a.m. to 5:00 p.m. and Sunday from noon to 5:00 p.m. Closed on Thanksgiving and Christmas through New Year's Day.

Fees

None

History

In 1978, the dream of two lifelong friends came true when Dauset Trails Nature Center opened its doors for the first time. Hampton Daughtry and David Settle shared a desire to preserve some of the natural terrain and indigenous wildlife of Jackson, Georgia, for future generations to enjoy. Out of that desire came Dauset Trails Nature Center, an educational and recreational facility designed to provide each visitor with a unique environmental experience. The center derives its name from parts of its founders' last names.

Size

1,100 acres

Features

Hike to your heart's content on more than six miles of trails which reveal surprises as you make your way through the rolling forestland. Discover beaver dams, log cabin ruins, wildlife, and wildflowers in season as the trails open up before you. The center offers environmental educational programs, bird-watching, natural

The tiny bird's-foot violet (Viola pedata) is one of the easiest violets to identify.

history exhibits, and an injured and orphaned animal exhibit. Some of the short-term animals in this exhibit can be rehabilitated, but the long-term residents are not able to be released into the wild.

Directions

From I-75, take Exit 65 (GA 36) and travel east toward Jackson for 2.9 miles until you reach High Falls Road. Turn right and travel 2.4 miles to Mount Vernon Church Road. Turn left and travel 3.1 miles. The entrance to the center is on the left.

Tips

Photographing wildlife and bird-watching are very popular here, so remember to bring your camera and binoculars. You may also wish to bring a picnic lunch, as picnic facilities are available on the grounds. Special programs for large groups must be arranged at least two months in advance. Camping, canoeing, and fishing are available to groups reserving the campground.

Accessibility

All of the center's facilities are accessible to disabled persons.

Side Trips

Located in Milledgeville, 46 miles southeast, is Lockerly Arboretum (pages 98–103). In Fort Valley, 75 miles southwest, is Massee Lane Gardens (pages 63–67). In Pine Mountain, located 75 miles to the northwest, is Callaway Gardens (pages 113–21).

Decorative garden accents such as this Japanese-style bench lend a personal touch to the gardens.

VINES BOTANICAL GARDENS

Address

3500 Oak Grove Road
Loganville, Georgia 30249-2236
770-466-7532

Hours

Open Tuesday through Sunday from 10:00 a.m. to 7:00 p.m. during daylight-saving time and from 10:00 a.m. to 5:00 p.m. the rest of the year. Call for holiday hours.

Fees

Yes. Discounts are available for senior citizens and children ages six to twelve. Children under age five are admitted free.

History

In 1979, Charles "Boe" and Myrna Adams purchased what is now Vines Botanical Gardens. Boe, an insurance executive, immediately set about improving the house and grounds. Exten-sive remodeling transformed the house from a typical 1970s two-story into an eighteen-thousand-square-foot mansion surrounded by twenty-five acres of elaborate gardens. The property was then suitable for the Adamses' lifestyle, which included extensive entertaining of friends and business associates. Most of the improvements to the property were completed by 1987.

The Adamses lived on the property with Myrna's father, Odie O. Vines, until 1990, when they moved back to their native Arkansas. At that time, they donated the property to Gwinnett County for use as public gardens. Named for Myrna's father, the gardens were turned over to the Vines Botanical Gardens Foundation, Inc., a nonprofit organization, in 1994. Its goal is to develop the property into one of the Southeast's garden treasures.

Size

90 acres, including 25 acres of gardens

Features

As you stroll around the beautifully landscaped gardens, you will delight at the variety of treasures. The sounds will be your first experience, as the fountains, the brook, and waterfowl harmonize a welcoming song. Upon entering the gardens, you will find that your other senses are exhilarated in turn as you make your way through the diverse and abundant plantings. Artfully incorporated into the gardens, which surround a 3½-acre lake, is a collection of antique statuary imported from Italy, Yugoslavia, and France.

Distinctive theme gardens demonstrate practical landscape uses for a variety of annuals, perennials, shrubs, and trees. These gardens include the Asian Garden, the White Garden, the Rose Garden, the Whimsical Garden, the Odie Vines Flower Garden, the Southscape Garden, the Woodland Terrace, the Brook Garden, and the Reflection Pool. Several are especially beautiful, particularly the Odie Vines Flower Garden, the White Garden, the Rose Garden, and the Brook Garden. The Odie Vines Flower Garden showcases a palette of colorful flowers almost year-round. The White Garden, enhanced with seasonal plantings of annuals

Ingenious cutouts in the pathway to the White Garden's gazebo create unusual planting sites for hostas.

83

and perennials, features varieties planted for their white flowers or whitish green foliage. This garden is especially breathtaking in the spring. Adjacent to the White Garden is the Rose Garden, where the profusion of blooms in late spring comes under the watchful eyes of four exquisite statues symbolizing the different seasons. The more than eighty varieties of Old Garden Roses are labeled with the roses' names and the year they were introduced into commerce. Across the lake from the Rose Garden is the Brook Garden, whose rocky stream winds through a collection of low-growing perennials and shrubs.

Other features include a demonstration area, a picnic area, the Vines Gift Shop, the Garden Room Restaurant, a botanical research library, and restrooms. The gift shop, restaurant, and library are located in the Vines House. Gardening programs and special events designed for children and adults are announced in the gardens' quarterly newsletter.

Directions

From I-20, take Exit 42 (GA 20 North/GA 138 East). Travel north on GA 20 for 16.5 miles; it makes a couple of turns, so pay close attention. Turn west (left) onto US 78/GA 10. Travel 1.1 miles to Brand Road and turn right. After 0.1 mile, turn left onto Oak Grove Road. Travel 0.8 mile. The entrance to the gardens is on the right.

Tips

Attractive any time of the year, the gardens are especially colorful in the spring when the azaleas are in bloom. The well-maintained pathways flow from one garden to another as gently as the stream which feeds the pond. Garden maps are available at the gatehouse. The ease of access makes these gardens particularly attractive to individuals with disabilities. Lunch is served Tuesday through Sunday from 11:30 a.m. to 2:30 p.m. at the Garden Room Restaurant, located on the second floor of the Vines House.

Accessibility

Particular attention has been paid to making most of the gardens and the building accessible to disabled persons.

Side Trips

Loganville is located midway between Athens and Atlanta, giving garden visitors a difficult choice of where to go next. There are three gardens in Athens (see pages 10–23) and five in Atlanta (see pages 25–43).

Statues representing the four seasons preside over the Rose Garden.

ROCK CITY GARDENS

Address
1400 Patten Road
Lookout Mountain, Georgia 30750-2621
706-820-2531

Hours
Open daily from 8:30 a.m. to sunset. Closed on Christmas. Hours may be extended during summer and special events.

Fees
Yes. Children two years and younger are admitted free. Group rates for twenty or more are available, as are special travel packages for families.

History
Long before preservation of the environment became a popular cause, Frieda Carter was preserving mountain wildflowers and native shrubs on a ten-acre rocky mountaintop in the northernmost corner of Georgia. She and her husband, Garnet Carter, had acquired the property in 1924 as part of a land-option deal for developing an exclusive three-hundred-acre tract on Lookout Mountain to be called Fairyland. Frieda, a musician and artist, was a quiet contrast to the cigar-smoking, smooth-talking Garnet, the entrepreneur who created the first miniature golf course. While he worked on real-estate developments and other ventures, she was busy in her wilderness gardens, marking pathways through the ancient and enormous rocky skyscrapers with a ball of twine. For more than six years, without interruption from Garnet, Frieda collected indigenous plants and relocated them in the protected crevices of the ancient promontory Garnet called "Rock City."

During the Great Depression, Garnet, no longer riding the boom of the real-estate market, became interested in Frieda's rocky gardens as a possible tourist attraction. At that time, Frieda was beginning to show signs of a debilitating disease that would eventually rob her of her mobility. Garnet's desire to assist his beloved Frieda

Rock, the building material of choice,
has been used extensively to create
beautiful and rustic gardens.

with her Rock City project, coupled with his unlimited optimism and business savvy, resulted in the creation of Rock City Gardens.

In 1932, in the middle of the Depression, the gardens opened to the public. Initially, they ex-perienced only minimal success. Garnet Carter's formula for a successful business venture had everything except the most important part–tourists. He knew that in order for business to improve, he had to do something special to spread the word about Rock City.

He sought the advice of Fred Maxwell, a friend and owner of an advertising company. The two of them eventually came upon the idea of painting slogans on barns along the more heavily used highways from the Gulf of Mexico to the Great Lakes. Fred Maxwell gave the barn-painting assignment to Clark Byers, a nineteen-year-old apprentice sign painter in his employ. Byers, taken aback at the idea of traveling around the country painting slogans on barns, asked, "Why, what would we paint on them?" Garnet Carter scribbled on a scrap of paper and slid the paper across his desk to Byers. Scrawled across the paper were three simple words des-

tined to become one of the most recognizable, most famous, and without a doubt most successful advertising slogans of all time: "See Rock City."

The year was 1935. Over the next thirty years, Clark Byers painted the slogan on more than nine hundred barns in nineteen states from Florida to the Canadian border. In the 1960s, during Lyndon B. Johnson's presidency, the "Lady Bird Act" banning certain billboard advertisements was passed, and the painted barns began to disappear. Most were torn down or painted over to comply with legislation. Only about one hundred barns survive today as historical landmarks sporting the simple invitation to "See Rock City."

Size
14 acres

Features
The list of features packed into this rugged mountaintop is seemingly endless. The ten acres of gardens, recognized by the Garden Club of America with the Bronze Medal of Distinction,

Steps spiraling down into the forest allow the wild gardens to unfold slowly.

A swinging bridge suspended above a ravine disappears into the autumn forest (next page).

are home to more than four hundred species of wildflowers, shrubs, and other plants native to the Georgia and Tennessee mountains. The self-guided trail traverses rocky terrain that is a geologist's heaven with earthly names: Needle's Eye, Mushroom Rock, Fat Man's Squeeze, and Balanced Rock. Lover's Leap, a rocky outcrop, affords a panoramic view of Virginia, Tennessee, Kentucky, North and South Carolina, Georgia, and Alabama—seven states in all. Children will delight in the Fairyland Caverns, Mother Goose Village, and the white fallow deer which roam Deer Park. Prospector's Point, open from Memorial Day to Labor Day, is perfect for finding gemstones.

One of the special events staged each year is the Fairy Tale Festival, complete with storytellers, puppeteers, and magic shows. During the Christmas season, the Enchanted Garden of Lights transforms the gardens into a well-lit winter wonderland with more than twenty holiday scenes. There are also creature comforts such as the Big Rock Cafe, Rocky's Stop Cookie Shop, Jim Garrahy's Fudge and Candy Kitchen, and gift and souvenir shops like the Wild West Emporium, the Christmas Shop, and the Cliff Terrace.

The rocky terrain provides a stark contrast to the beautiful native gardens.

Directions

The gardens, located about 6 miles from Chattanooga, Tennessee, on top of Lookout Mountain, are easy to find from most interstate highways in the area, as the exits are well marked. Just follow the signs to Rock City Gardens.

Tips

Rock City Gardens is open year-round, but to enjoy the mountain wildflowers and other flowering indigenous plants at their peak, plan ahead by calling. You may want to inquire about the various special events scheduled throughout the year. Allow approximately an hour and a half to walk the self-guided trail.

Accessibility

Due to the rocky terrain, accessibility for disabled persons is limited. An abbreviated tour of the park is conducted for individuals with special needs.

Side Trips

Located 70 miles southeast of Lookout Mountain is Adairsville, home of Barnsley Gardens at Woodlands (pages 3–9). In Mount Berry, 90 miles southeast, is Oak Hill at the Martha Berry Museum (pages 106–11) .

GUIDO GARDENS

Address

P.O. Box 508
Metter, Georgia 30439-0508
912-685-2222

Hours

The gardens and chapel never close. Studio tours are conducted Monday through Friday from 8:00 a.m. to 5:00 p.m.

Fees

None

History

Guido Gardens is home to the Sower Studio, where Dr. Michael A. Guido produces radio broadcasts and telecasts which are aired worldwide. Twice each year for four days, the gardens provide a spectacular backdrop for taping the Sower telecasts. Developed more than twenty-five years ago, the gardens are continually expanding and evolving due to the generosity of McCorkle Nurseries in Dearing, Georgia.

The nondenominational Guido Evangelistic Association, Inc., was founded and is directed by Dr. Guido, who each day delivers a simple message of salvation to more than thirty million homes. His message, given in humorous, anecdotal fashion, is provided free of charge to radio and television stations.

Dr. Guido and his wife, Audrey, started their ministry by vowing to never ask for money or try to sell their viewers or listeners anything. A noble vow, but how does one go about establishing a worldwide ministry without asking for money? Through prayer and a strong belief in the word of Jesus Christ. Their prayers eventually led them to the small Georgia farming town of Metter. Here, an answered prayer for a place to begin their broadcast ministry came in the form of an offer of a small lot from the mayor. Located at the edge of the quiet little town, the small lot is today the home of one of the most successful broadcast ministries in the world. The radio and television broadcasts, entitled *A Seed for the Garden of Your Heart*, bring God's word to audiences everywhere.

Size
3½ acres

Features
Expertly planted and maintained, Guido Gardens showcases a wide array of native Georgia plants, including pines, dogwoods, and lots of azaleas. Other features include the Chapel in the Pines, fountains, a gazebo adjacent to the Water Garden, and strategically placed benches designed to give the visitor the best possible view. All of this is accompanied by inspirational music, which helps set the tone for a most enjoyable visit.

Directions

From I-16, take Exit 23 (GA 23/121) and travel north on GA 121 (North Lewis Street) for 3 miles. The entrance is on the right at 600 North Lewis Street.

Tips

Designed for year-round use, the gardens can be visited in any season, but the spring blooms are usually the most spectacular. Nights of Lights, a Christmas-season spectacular with more than two hundred thousand lights, begins at Thanksgiving and runs until New Year's Day.

Accessibility

All of the facilities at the gardens are accessible to disabled persons.

Side Trips

In Statesboro, 35 miles northeast, is Georgia Southern Botanical Garden (pages 156–57). Seven gardens and the historic Savannah squares are located 65 miles southeast in Savannah (see pages 124–55).

> Soothing sounds emanating from the fountains and trickling brooks help encourage visitors to stop and meditate.

LOCKERLY ARBORETUM

Address

1534 Irwinton Road
Milledgeville, Georgia 31061-3827
912-452-2112

Hours

Open Monday through Friday from 8:30 a.m. to
4:30 p.m. and Saturday from 1:00 p.m. to 5:00 p.m.

Fees

None

History

In 1965, Edward J. Grassman, a New Jersey native and avid amateur naturalist and ornithologist, provided the initial funds from his company, Georgia Kaolin, to purchase and fence the property that was to become Lockerly Arboretum. The origin of the name Lockerly— taken from Lockerly Hall, the antebellum manor house adjacent to the arboretum—has been lost through the generations. Grassman had established Georgia Kaolin in 1927 in Dry Branch, with a sister plant in Washington County, after the kaolin—a fine white clay used in the manufacture of china, paint, plastic, paper, and paper coatings—found in Virginia proved to be of poor quality.

The Lockerly Arboretum Foundation, Inc., was chartered in New Jersey by Carl Vinson, a member of the foundation's first board of trustees. The foundation was chartered in New Jersey because Georgia limits the life of such charters. Since the plants at the arboretum will endure for many generations, it was necessary for the foundation, which is solely responsible for operating and maintaining the arboretum, to exist indefinitely. Permanence in a nonprofit organization is paramount to attracting support.

At the time Lockerly was established, Grassman

was very specific as to its mission. It was to edu-cate students, young and old, enhance their knowledge, and give them practical experience they could share with others. He was adamant that sound horticultural practices be followed, with minimal reliance on pesticides and an emphasis on organic principles. Grassman died in 1973 at the age of eighty-five, leaving Georgians, particularly the residents of Milledgeville, a won-derful legacy of living beauty.

Size
47 acres

Features

This is the perfect place to see more than six thousand plant species. To really experience the arboretum, travel on foot via the well-main-tained trails. If you are less adventurous, you don't even have to leave your vehicle. Some of the collections you will see contain rhododen-dron, native and hybrid azaleas, hawthorns, hostas, ferns, hollies, camellias, pieris, vibur-nums, conifers, daylilies, herbs, and grasses. Other features include a sand tracking bed, which shows the footprints of different animals; a gazebo; a spring-fed pond displaying shore, bog, and aquatic plants; the Woods Museum; the Tropical Greenhouse; the Desert Greenhouse; the Iris and Butterfly Garden; a vineyard; a berry bramble; a developing climax forest; and the Sand Hills Collection of plants and Southern indica azaleas.

The arboretum's signpost leaves no doubt that there is plenty to see and do.

Directions

From I-20, take Exit 51 (US 441 South) and travel 30 miles to Milledgeville. In Milledgeville, US 441 South becomes Columbia Street. Turn left onto Hancock Street, travel 4 blocks, and turn right onto Wayne Street (US 441 South Business), which becomes Irwinton Road just outside the city limits. The entrance to the arboretum is on the left at 1534 Irwinton Road.

Tips

Just driving through the arboretum will take you about fifteen minutes, but a walking trip is highly recommended, particularly in the spring when the woodland wildflowers are blooming. Maps are available at the office; you are encouraged to return them when you finish your visit so they may be recycled to the next visitor. Guided tours for groups can be arranged by calling in advance. It is important to remember that the arboretum is primarily a teaching and research facility, which accounts for the absence of tourist-type features such as a gift shop and cafe.

Sacred lotus (Nelumbium nucifera) nearly bursting into bloom skirt the edge of a pond (previous page).

Accessibility

A circular drive through the arboretum makes it almost entirely accessible by vehicle. Disabled persons may require some assistance when using the restroom facilities.

Side Trips

Dauset Trails Nature Center (pages 78–79) is located about 46 miles northwest in Jackson. Located in the same general vicinity are the Melvin L. Newman Wetlands Center (pages 70–71) in Hampton and the William H. Reynolds Nature Preserve (pages 104–5) in Morrow.

The arboretum is laced with nature trails lined with native and imported species.

WILLIAM H. REYNOLDS NATURE PRESERVE

Address

5665 Reynolds Road
Morrow, Georgia 30260-3731
404-961-9257

Hours

The preserve is open daily from 8:30 a.m. to sunset. The Interpretive Center is open Monday through Friday from 8:30 a.m. to 5:30 p.m.

Fees

Donations are accepted.

History

William Huie Reynolds was a man of many talents and loves. He was a self-taught attorney who served as a state representative and a judge. Later in life, his interests shifted toward more private endeavors, like protecting the forests on his farm and collecting native species of azaleas. In 1976, Judge Reynolds donated his cherished forests and wetlands to Clayton County. The preserve named in his honor was dedicated in 1977. He died in 1984 at the age of ninety-seven.

Size

130 acres

Features

Georgia Native Plants Trail is wheelchair-accessible. Other trails are laid out in half-mile loops, for a total of four miles through the woods and wetlands. The Interpretive Center displays local wildlife in a natural habitat. Other features include the Heritage Vegetable Garden, the Herb Garden, a compost demonstration site, and some nineteenth-century farm equipment.

Directions

From I-75, take Exit 76 (GA 54), travel north for 0.9 mile to Reynolds Road, and turn left. The preserve entrance is on the left at 1 mile.

Accessibility

Some trails are paved and allow easy access. Elderly and disabled individuals may require assistance on other trails.

Tips

Emphasis is placed on preserving and reintroducing native plant materials, especially wildflowers, so remember to bring a wildflower guide, a camera, and kneepads. There is a lot of water in this preserve. Mosquitoes may be a problem in the summer, so come prepared.

Side Trips

In Hampton, 23 miles south, is the Melvin L. Newman Wetlands Center (page 70–71). In Stockbridge, 20 miles southeast, is Panola Mountain State Conservation Park (pages 158–59). In Fairburn, 29 miles southwest, is Cochran Mill Nature Center and Arboretum (pages 60–61).

Oak Hill at the Martha Berry Museum

Address

189 Mount Berry Station

Mount Berry, Georgia 30149-0189

706-291-1883

Hours

Open Tuesday through Saturday from 10:00 a.m. to 5:00 p.m. and Sunday from 1:00 p.m. to 5:00 p.m. Closed on Monday, New Year's Eve, New Year's Day, the Fourth of July, Thanksgiving, Christmas Eve, and Christmas Day. Appointments at other times can be arranged by calling the museum.

Fees

Yes. Discounts are available for children, groups, and AAA members. Children under six years of age are admitted free of charge.

History

Martha McChesney Berry, born in 1866, was the second-oldest of Frances Rhea Berry and Captain Thomas Berry's eight children. Martha's family didn't suffer the financial ruin that plagued many Southern families after the Civil War, due to her father's pledge to his Northern creditors to settle his debts before war broke out. Because of his pledge, Captain Berry was able to secure credit from Northern bankers after the war.

In 1859, Captain Berry purchased Oak Hill as a home for his bride-to-be. Shortly after arriving at Oak Hill, Frances began the gardens, starting with the Formal Boxwood Garden, which she often called the "Big Garden." Martha, who shared her mother's love of gardens, contributed the Sunken Garden to her mother's plan in the early 1930s.

Martha enjoyed the gardens, but her passion in life was to educate the children who lived in the surrounding communities. She began a school with three students in a tiny log cabin on eighty-three acres bequeathed to her by her

Originally a playhouse for the Berry children, the cabin was used by Martha Berry as her first school.

father. From these humble beginnings grew what survives today as Berry College. The college owns more than twenty-six thousand acres, making it one of the largest campuses in the world.

Built in 1847, Oak Hill was purchased by Captain Thomas Berry in 1859.

Size

170 acres

Features

Opened to the public in 1972, the gardens of Oak Hill provide a fitting botanical complement to the historic mansion. Featured are the Formal Boxwood Garden, the Sunken Garden, the Hillside Garden, the Goldfish Garden, the Sundial Garden, Azalea Trail, the Bridal Walk, and the Wildflower Meadow. The Formal Boxwood Garden, accented with seasonal plants and annuals, was one of the first gardens Frances Berry planted after her marriage. The Sunken Garden, sometimes referred to as the Terrace Garden, features flowering Kwanzan cherry trees, a gift to Martha Berry from the emperor of Japan in 1932. More than 140 varieties of daylilies are planted under the cherry trees, which are usually in full bloom by April. Azalea Trail is planted with more than 400 native azaleas, which explode into bloom during the first week of April. Also featured is a mile-long nature trail which ambles through a forest abundantly carpeted in places with lush ferns. A pond teeming with fish is located at the edge of the Wildflower Meadow. Other features at Oak Hill are the Martha Berry Museum and Art Gallery, the Walkway of Life, the original log-cabin playhouse used as the first school, and a gift shop.

Under Martha Berry's direction, the
Terrace Garden, complete with
fountain, was developed in 1932.

This fountain, cast in France, graced
the front of an Alabama hotel before
it was given to Martha Berry.

Directions

From I-75, take Exit 126 (US 411) and travel west for 27 miles to GA 1 Loop North. Travel 7.8 miles to the Oak Hill entrance, on the left.

Tips

The gardens at Oak Hill, one of only four All-American Selections Display Gardens in Georgia, start blooming about the middle of March and continue though most of the year. A variety of programs and special events is hosted at Oak Hill, so call for a program guide. A tour of the museum and home is recommended in order to set the stage for a more complete appreciation of the gardens and Martha Berry. Also recommended is a drive through the campus of Berry College, located adjacent to Oak Hill.

Accessibility

Designated parking is available. The first floors of the buildings are accessible to disabled persons. Paved pathways provide access to parts of the gardens.

Side Trips

Barnsley Gardens at Woodlands (pages 3–9) is 20 miles northeast in Adairsville. Sixty-five miles southeast in Roswell is Chattahoochee Nature Center (pages 122–23). Ninety miles to the north in Lookout Mountain is Rock City Gardens (pages 86–93).

A vine-covered alcove decorated with cascades of impatiens awaits the garden visitor.

CALLAWAY GARDENS

Address

P.O. Box 2000
Pine Mountain, Georgia 31822-2000
800-282-8181

Hours

Open daily from 7:00 a.m. to 7:00 p.m. from May through September. Hours at other times may vary depending on the season or scheduled events.

Fees

Yes. Per-family vehicle rates apply. Special rates are offered for individuals, commercial groups, and children. Rates may vary according to the season.

Golden yellow daffodils, a member of the narcissus family, are a recognizable harbinger of spring.

History

Cason J. Callaway, born in LaGrange, Georgia, in 1894 to Fuller and Ida Jane Cason Callaway, accomplished a great deal in his lifetime. He originated the Georgia Better Farms Movement and was a textile magnate, a president of the American Cotton Manufacturers Association, a director of U.S. Steel, a regent of the University of Georgia, owner-operator of Blue Springs Farm, and a lieutenant in the navy during World War I. But he is best remembered for his contribution to water recreation and the preservation and development of the Blue Springs and Barnes Creek watersheds–better known as Callaway Gardens.

Callaway began his textile career in 1911 at the age of seventeen, sweeping floors in his father's cotton mill in LaGrange. He later established Valley Waste Mills, which manufactured rags from cotton-mill waste. This innovative concept helped him make a name for himself in the textile industry.

The Pioneer Log Cabin, built in the
1830s from hand-hewn yellow pine logs,
was moved to the gardens in 1960.

A multitude of tropical butterflies
can be seen at the Cecil B. Day
Butterfly Conservatory.

In 1935, he turned the family textile business over to Earle Fuller Callaway, Jr., his younger brother, in order to embark on a different path with his wife of fifteen years, Virginia Hollis Hand Callaway. Together, Cason and Virginia created Callaway Gardens, which opened to the public on May 21, 1952. Cason died in 1961, and the Ida Cason Callaway Foundation received the gardens from Blue Springs Farm.

Size

2,500-acre display garden

Features

Callaway Gardens was designed to provide entertainment for every member of the family, and it more than delivers. Myriad activities are available throughout the year in an extraordinarily picturesque setting which showcases more than 750 varieties of azaleas. An abundance of this popular shrub is featured in the Azalea Bowl. Exhibits which show mother nature at her best, with a helping hand from mankind, are the John A. Sibley Horticultural Center, a complex of 5 acres of greenhouse and gardens planted with seasonal varieties and established collections of azaleas, camellias, and citrus; the Cecil B. Day Butterfly Center, a 4½-acre garden/conservatory in the Meadowlark Garden planted to attract butterflies and hummingbirds; and Mr. Cason's Vegetable Garden, the

The Azalea Bowl, planted with native and hybrid varieties, is one of the highlights on Azalea Trail.

Southern location for the Public Broadcasting Service series *The Victory Garden*.

Visitors enjoy such activities as hiking, bicycling, and birding on Azalea Trail, the 7.5-mile Discovery Bicycle Trail, the 1.5-mile Fit Trail, Laurel Spring Trail, Rhododendron Trail, Holly Trail, Wildflower Trail, and Mountain Creek Trail. If you would rather enjoy nature from your vehicle, there is the 5-mile Scenic Drive. Other features include Robin Lake Beach, the Ida Cason Callaway Memorial Chapel, the Vegetable Garden Shop, the Pioneer Log Cabin, and the Overlook Pavilion. Those interested in outdoor activities such as golf, tennis, racquetball, fishing, skeet shooting, and trapshooting will be pleased to find facilities at their disposal and equipment available for rent. There are also seven restaurants, gift shops, a pro shop, a tennis center, picnic tables, and restrooms.

Unique horticultural displays are a must-see at the John A. Sibley Horticultural Center (previous page).

Directions

From I-85 South from Atlanta, travel to I-185 South and take Exit 14. Turn left onto US 27 and travel 11 miles to Callaway Gardens. The entrance is on the right. From I-85 North from Columbus, take the GA 18 East Exit, travel 18 miles to US 27, turn right, and cross GA 354. The entrance is on the right.

Tips

A variety of programs, festivals, and special events, including the PGA's Buick Southern Open Golf Tournament and the Master's Water-Ski Championships, is planned throughout the year, so it is wise to call or write for a program guide. Lodging is available. Bicycles can be rented to tour the gardens, but most areas can be reached by car or tram. The azaleas for which the gardens are known begin blooming in late March or early April.

Accessibility

Designated parking is available. Most facilities are accessible to disabled persons.

Side Trips

Atlanta, which has five gardens (see pages 25–43), is 70 miles north. Massee Lane Gardens (pages 63–67) is 90 miles east in Fort Valley.

Miles and miles of nature
trails meander through
Callaway Gardens.

Chattahoochee Nature Center

Address

9135 Willeo Road
Roswell, Georgia 30075-4723
770-992-2055

Hours

Open Monday through Saturday from 9:00 a.m. to 5:00 p.m. and Sunday from noon to 5:00 p.m. Closed Thanksgiving, Christmas, and New Year's Day.

Fees

Yes. Discounts are available for children.

History

The site of Chattahoochee Nature Center was once the home of Cherokee Indians, who lived along the riverbanks in harmony with nature and treasured the land as their ultimate provider. This changed in the 1830s, when land lotteries brought white settlers onto land the Indians had been forced to leave. William and Mary Kelpen, former North Carolinians, brought their family, which eventually included six children, to settle this piece of rich bottom land. The Kelpens farmed the land, planting mostly cotton and fruit trees, and became an integral part of the Roswell community. William served as a Democratic county officer and as a justice of the peace.

Kelpen Farm was later home to the Horace Holden family until it was purchased for use as a preserve through the efforts of John Ripley Forbes and the National Science for Youth Foundation in 1976. Originally seven acres, the center has grown one small tract at a time. Today, the former home of the Cherokees, the Kelpens, and the Holdens is home to native plants and a variety of wildlife.

Size

127 acres

Features

The center features the Native Plants Garden, the Fern Garden, the Bog Garden, Woodland Nature Trail, Wildflower Trail, a boardwalk that winds through marshland and along the Chattahoochee River, a well-stocked nature store specializing in supplies for naturalists of all ages, and natural history exhibits. The most impressive of the natural history exhibits is the Birds of Prey Aviary, which features indigenous raptors that, because of serious injury, cannot be released back into the wild. Woodland Nature Trail takes the visitor through wooded uplands and along the banks of a pond frequented by numerous waterfowl.

Directions

From I-75, take Exit 113 (GA 120 Loop East), travel 1.2 miles, and exit to GA 120 East (Roswell Road Northeast). Travel 6.2 miles to Willeo Road, turn right, and travel 0.9 mile. The entrance to the center is on the right.

Tips

The success of the nature center's community outreach program is particularly evident on weekdays, when schoolchildren of all ages can be found in nearly every nook and cranny. If you are seeking peace and quiet, you may want to call ahead of time to avoid the hustle and bustle of an elementary-school field trip. Educating the com-

munity to the importance of the natural world is part of the mission of the center. To that end, it offers guided walks on Saturday and Sunday from 1:00 p.m. to 3:00 p.m.

Accessibility

All facilities except Woodland Nature Trail are accessible to disabled persons.

Side Trips

Elachee Nature Science Center (pages 68–69) is located 40 miles northeast in Gainesville. Oak Hill at the Martha Berry Museum (pages 106–11) is 57 miles northwest in Mount Berry. Barnsley Gardens at Woodlands (pages 3–9) is located 62 miles northwest in Adairsville.

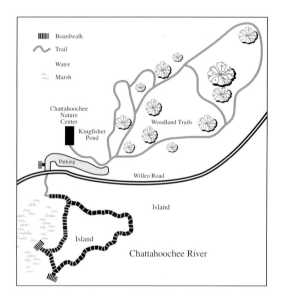

ANDREW LOW HOUSE

Address
329 Abercorn Street
Savannah, Georgia 31401-4634
912-233-6854

Hours
Open from 10:30 a.m. to 4:00 p.m. on Monday, Tuesday, Wednesday, Friday, and Saturday and from noon to 4:00 p.m. on Sundays. Closed Thursday and all major holidays.

Fees
Yes. Discounts are available.

History
Andrew Low, wealthy cotton merchant and future father-in-law of Juliette Gordon Low, built the house in 1848 for his wife, Sarah, and their young family. Designed by New York architect John Norris, the house has a West Indian influence. It is now the headquarters of the Georgia Colonial Dames, who purchased it in 1928. Juliette Gordon Low, who founded the Girl Scouts of America in 1912, owned the house until her death on January 17, 1927, at the age of sixty-six.

Size
¼ acre

Features
The house is a spectacular centerpiece for the two gardens on this historic property. One is in front. The other, a walled garden, hugs the house on three sides. The front garden duplicates the original design. Historical information regarding the walled garden is sketchy; it refers to a walled garden with camellias. Other features include dogwood trees, azaleas, camellias, and seasonal plantings.

Directions
From I-95, take Exit 17 (I-16) and travel east until the interstate ends at Montgomery Street. Be prepared to make an almost immediate right turn onto West Charlton Street. Travel past Pulaski and Madison Squares. The house is on the left facing Lafayette Square.

General Robert E. Lee was a guest at the Andrew Low House during his visit to Savannah.

Tips

The house tour lasts about thirty minutes and is recommended for those who want to fully appreciate the gardens. Parking in the historic district may be difficult; parking spaces along the streets are at a premium, and public parking fills quickly. Self-guided walking tours and guided tours are recommended. Tour maps and brochures are available at the visitor center.

Accessibility

The gardens are accessible to disabled persons, but the house is not.

Side Trips

The area boasts six other gardens and the historic Savannah squares (see pages 127–55).

CHATHAM COUNTY GARDEN CENTER AND BOTANICAL GARDENS

Address

1388 Eisenhower Drive
Savannah, Georgia 31406-3902
912-355-3883

Hours

The gardens are open daily from sunrise to sunset. The center is open Monday through Friday from 10:00 a.m. to 2:00 p.m.

Fees

Donations are accepted. Tours of the house and gardens are conducted by members of the garden council for a minimal fee.

George, the resident swan, adds a touch of elegance to the relatively young gardens.

History

After four years of negotiating with local government, the Savannah Area Council of Garden Clubs obtained a long-term lease on property once used by Chatham County as a prison farm. The Old Brown Farm, as it was called, was turned over to the council, a non-profit organization, in 1991 to be developed as gardens that would educate the public about plants which flourish under local conditions. The historic Helmken Street farmhouse, slated for demolition, was donated to the garden council by the county. In October 1992, the council moved it to the property. The restored structure now houses a garden research library and some artifacts. In 1993, the gardens opened unofficially to the public. The grand opening was held in May 1997.

The farmhouse was moved to the gardens instead of being razed to make way for a new road.

Size
10½ acres

Features
You would never suspect these lovely gardens were once a prison farm. The old farmhouse,

mature trees, and an eye-catching landscape suggest permanence. Adding to the landscape are several gardens maintained by volunteers from area garden clubs. Featured are the Azalea and Camellia Garden, the Native Plant Garden, the Kitchen Garden, the Herb Parterre, the Perennial Garden, the Four Seasons Garden, the Rose Garden, the Shade Garden, and the Children's Garden. Other features include a pond, nature trails, a pine and sweetgum forest, a mixed hardwood forest, and wildflower meadows. There is also an archaeological dig on the property.

Directions

From I-95, take Exit 16 (GA 204/Abercorn Street) and travel east for 11.3 miles to Eisenhower Drive. Turn right and travel 1.3 miles. The entrance to the gardens is on the left at McCorkle Drive.

Tips

Visit the gardens during the week, when the center is open. That way, you may start your visit with a tour of the restored 1840s farmhouse. The impressive Rose Garden usually peaks around the middle or end of April. You may want to call the center for blooming times.

Zinnias of assorted colors accent the Kitchen Garden at the rear of the farmhouse.

Accessibility

Designated parking is available. The first floor of the center is accessible to disabled persons. The gardens at the rear of the center have paved pathways.

Side Trips

The area boasts six other gardens and the historic Savannah squares (see pages 124–25 and 130–55).

COASTAL GARDENS

Address

2 Canebrake Road
Savannah, Georgia 31419-9298
912-921-5460

Hours

Open daily from sunrise to sunset. The office is open Monday through Friday from 8:00 a.m. to 4:00 p.m.

Fees

None

History

Three small bamboo plants acquired in 1890 by Mrs. H. B. Miller from a Cuban rice grower living near Georgia's Ogeechee River started it all. Mrs. Miller planted the tiny plants on the farm she shared with her brothers. More than one hundred years later, these three plants have become two acres of giant Japanese timber bamboo.

As Mrs. Miller's plants grew on the "Bamboo Farm," as it became known, the grove was brought to the attention of Dr. David Fairchild, head of the United States Department of Agriculture's Seed and Plant Introduction Section in Washington, D.C. Dr. Fairchild had studied bamboo in Java with another American, Barbour Lathrop. He interested Lathrop in the Bamboo Farm to the point that Lathrop bought the entire forty-six acres and gave them to the Plant Introduction Section of the USDA. The farm was officially accepted by a 1919 act of Congress.

The farm, renamed the Barbour Lathrop Plant Introduction Garden by the USDA, enjoyed sixty years of prosperity as an integral part of the Plant Introduction Section. Plant material from all over the world was received at the farm and evaluated to determine its suitability to the Savannah climate. If the plants thrived, they were shipped to similar climates all over the United States. Thanks to the influx of so many exotic plant species for so many years, the farm is home to a number of rare trees and shrubs. Unfortunately, the farm was closed in 1978 as a cost-containment measure. It remained

Japanese timber bamboo
is the largest of the
bamboo species.

Bamboo henon (Phyllostachys nigra) is 1 of more than 180 bamboo species at the garden (previous page).

The mute swan (Cygnus olor) has a loud, trumpeting call that is rarely heard.

closed until 1983, when the University of Georgia Cooperative Extension Service acquired the property and renamed it the Coastal Area Extension Center.

Since 1983, it has served the community by conducting demonstration projects related to coastal agricultural practices. It also provided visiting giant pandas with bamboo leaves during the time when the Chinese government permitted them to travel to zoos in North America. Since 1989, harvested bamboo leaves have fed red pandas, an endangered species kept in American zoos. Coastal Gardens, as it is now called, has the distinction of being the oldest remaining bamboo farm in the United States. It boasts more than 180 different species of bamboo, including rare species not found anywhere else in the country.

Size
46 acres

Features
These incredible gardens have a great deal to offer the plant enthusiast. Known for their extensive collection of bamboo, they also feature display gardens of herbs, annuals, and perennials; turf plots; the Vegetable Garden; a grape arbor; a pear orchard; strawberry fields; cropland; a blackberry bramble; a compost exhibit; a weather station; greenhouses; the Lakes and Aquatic Garden; the Rose and Daylily Garden; and, of course, a shade bamboo collection which includes a bamboo forest. Some of the other botanical collections are the Persimmon Collection, the Christmas Tree Collection, and the Magnolia Collection. Also on the premises are the Barbour Lathrop Bamboo Gardens, a gift shop, a conference center, and a bamboo artifacts exhibit.

Directions
From I-95, take Exit 16 (GA 204), travel east for 1.7 miles, and exit to US 17. Travel south for 1.1 miles. The entrance to the gardens is on the right.

Tips
During strawberry season, the gardens open their fields to the public to pick strawberries; there is a charge. On Sunday, a local church uses the conference center for its weekly worship services.

Accessibility
Most of the gardens are easily accessed by vehicle. Designated parking is available for disabled person. Some areas of the gardens near the conference center have paved walkways accessed by ramps.

Side Trips
The area boasts six other gardens and the historic Savannah squares (see pages 124–29 and 136–55).

FORSYTH PARK

Address
Park and Tree Commission
P.O. Box 1027
Savannah, Georgia 31402-1027
912-651-6610

Hours
The park is always open.

Fees
None

History
Sometimes referred to as the "Last Square," Forsyth Park was designed by William Bishoff, a native of Bavaria, for the property's original owner, William Hodgson. Hodgson Park, as it was once called, was opened to the public by Hodgson and kept open at his expense. In 1851, the park was renamed for John Forsyth, governor of Georgia and secretary of state under Presidents Andrew Jackson and Martin Van Buren. Around the time the park was renamed, it was acquired by the city. The James Beebe Company of New York was engaged to build the fountain, whose design was taken from a fountain exhibited at the Crystal Palace in London in 1851. In 1866, the park's size was doubled thanks to the addition of the Forsyth Park Extension.

Size
21 acres

Features
The ornate fountain near the center of the park has an identical twin in Cuzco, Peru. Added to the park in 1858, the fountain has recently undergone a restoration paid for by the people of Savannah. Other features at the park are a jogging track, a basketball court, tennis courts, a playground, benches, azaleas, magnolias, palmettos, oak trees dripping with Spanish moss, the Fragrance Garden for the Blind, and a memorial commemorating Savannah's Confederate soldiers.

The detailed figures in Forsyth Park's distinctive fountain are a favorite among visitors to Savannah.

137

Directions

From I-95, take Exit 17 (I-16) and travel east until the interstate dead-ends into Montgomery Street. Turn right onto West Liberty Street, across from the visitor center, travel 0.3 mile to Bull Street, and turn right. At 0.5 mile, Bull Street dead-ends at West Gaston Street. The park is directly ahead.

Tips

This popular park is beautifully planted. Even after the azaleas and magnolias are finished blooming, it is a wonderful place to relax. The fountain is a favorite Savannah landmark. If you enjoy feeding the not-so-wild wildlife, you can share your lunch with a willing squirrel or two and several dozen pigeons.

Accessibility

Designated parking and sidewalks provide easy access for disabled persons.

Side Trips

The area boasts six other gardens and the historic Savannah squares (see pages 124–35 and 140–55).

The twin of the beautiful cast-iron fountain can be found in Cuzco, Peru.

ISAIAH DAVENPORT HOUSE MUSEUM

Address

324 East State Street
Savannah, Georgia 31401-3411
912-236-8097

Hours

Open daily from 10:00 a.m. to 4:30 p.m. Closed on all major holidays.

Fees

Yes. Children under six are admitted free. No admission is charged to enter the garden or the gift shop.

History

In 1955, this once-stately house nearly fell to a developer's desire to furnish Savannah with another parking lot. The house, an excellent example of the Federal style, was completed in 1820 by Isaiah Davenport, a Rhode Island native and master builder. Davenport served

as a Savannah city alderman before dying in 1827 during a yellow fever outbreak.

During the 1920s and 1930s, the historic home deteriorated into a tenement house. Eventually, it was more valuable, at least to some, as a pile of old bricks. When demolition seemed imminent, seven determined women raised the money to purchase and restore the old house, which opened as a museum in 1963. These same ladies established the Historic Savannah Foundation, which has saved over seventeen hundred historically significant properties.

Size
⅛ acre

Features
The garden is not original to the house. It was added to the property in 1976 by the Savannah Trustees' Garden Club as its bicentennial project. During 1996, the garden plantings were

Isaiah Davenport House Museum faces Columbia Square, which was laid out in 1799.

revitalized and a fountain was added. The horticultural features include azaleas, boxwoods, perennials, and plantings of seasonal annuals. A museum shop is on the garden level.

Directions
From I-95, take Exit 17 (I-16) and travel east until the interstate dead-ends into Montgomery Street. Follow Montgomery Street for 0.3 mile and turn right onto West Oglethorpe Avenue. Travel 0.6 mile to Habersham Street and turn left. Travel 0.1 mile to the other side of Columbia Square. The house is on the corner of Habersham and East State Streets.

Tips
Tours begin on the hour and the half-hour. The last tour is at 4:00 p.m. Proceeds from sales in the gift shop support preservation projects of the Historic Savannah Foundation.

Accessibility
Only the garden level of the house, where restroom facilities are located, is accessible to disabled persons.

Side Trips
The area boasts six other gardens and the historic Savannah squares (see pages 124–39 and 143–55).

The piazza and a fourth floor
were added to the Juliette
Gordon Low Birthplace in 1886.

JULIETTE GORDON LOW BIRTHPLACE

Address
142 Bull Street
Savannah, Georgia 31401-3723
912-233-4501

Hours
Open Monday, Tuesday, Thursday, Friday, and Saturday from 10:00 a.m. to 4:00 p.m. and Sunday from 12:30 p.m. to 4:30 p.m. Closed Wednesday, Christmas Eve, Christmas Day, New Year's Eve, New Year's Day, and St. Patrick's Day.

Fees
Yes. Group rates are available.

History
The house where Juliette Gordon Low was born was finished in 1821 for James Wayne. As was the tradition of the day, a formal walled garden was added. In 1831, Wayne sold the house to his niece Sarah Gordon, Juliette's grandmother. In 1886, the piazza was added, and a fence replaced the wall. The garden's formal design evolved into a tropical style. In 1930, the garden was turned into a playground. In 1956, the Girl Scouts of America purchased the house from the Gordon family and reclaimed the garden with a parterre design by landscape architect Clermont Lee. The house was Savannah's first registered National Historical Landmark.

Size
1/8 acre

Features
The Victorian Garden is easily accessed through the iron courtyard gate and is visible from the curved piazza. Pathways of crushed oyster shells outline the symmetrical beds, which feature azaleas, flowering almonds, white crape myrtles, leatherleaf mahonia, camellias, bananas, and common pomegranate.

Directions

From I-95, take Exit 17 (I-16) and travel east until the interstate dead-ends into Montgomery Street. At 0.3 mile, turn right onto West Oglethorpe Avenue. Travel 0.3 mile to Bull Street. The house is at the corner.

Tips

The birthplace is very busy during school breaks. Street parking is scarce, so you may wish to walk from public parking.

Accessibility

Disabled persons should call prior to their visit, as there is only one designated parking space. Access to the house is limited, but a "scalamobile" can be set up with advance notice. The restroom is accessible to disabled persons.

Side Trips

The area boasts six other gardens and the historic Savannah squares (see pages 124–41 and 146–55).

Bronze cranes from one of the Chinese Imperial Gardens were a gift of the first Girl Scout leader.

Owens-Thomas House
of the Telfair Museum
# of Art

Address

124 Abercorn Street
Savannah, Georgia 31401-3732
912-233-9743

Hours

Open Tuesday through Saturday from 10:00 a.m. to 5:00 p.m. Open Sunday and Monday from 2:00 p.m. to 5:00 p.m. Closed January and major holidays.

Fees

Yes. Discounts are available for students and children twelve years old and under.

History

Situated at the northeast side of Oglethorpe Square, the Owens-Thomas House is one of the finest examples of Regency architecture in the United States. Designed by English architect William Jay and built between 1816 and 1819, the private residence was commissioned by Richard Richardson, a prominent Savannah banker and cotton merchant. Frances Bolton Richardson, Richard's wife, was related to William Jay by marriage, which may have had some influence on Richardson's decision to commission the twenty-five-year-old architect. Richardson was also influenced by Jay's British demeanor and style, so much so that he retained Jay to design and construct a branch of the United States Bank.

In 1822, Savannah suffered fires and an outbreak of yellow fever. Richardson felt the suffering acutely, due to the death of his wife and an economic depression. Shortly after Frances's death, Richardson lost the house to creditors. The structure was then used for a short time as a boardinghouse, one respectable enough to house the Marquis de Lafayette during his visit to Savannah in 1825. It is said that Lafayette addressed a crowd from the balcony of the boardinghouse. In 1830, the house was purchased by George Welchman Owens, whose granddaughter Margaret Thomas bequeathed it to the Telfair Academy of Arts and Sciences in 1951 for use as a museum. The name Owens-Thomas is used to honor Margaret Thomas's father and grandfather.

Size
¹/₈ acre

Features
A walled garden installed in the former stable yard during a 1950s renovation transports visitors back to the early 1800s. The walls are partially covered with vines, and short, immaculately clipped boxwood borders skirt the garden beds. The inviting sounds of water droplets breaking the surface of a small pool help keep the present at bay as you walk along the stone pathways. The Parterre Garden utilizes a variety of plants that thrive in the moderate Savannah climate, such as azaleas, nandinas, leatherleaf mahonia, junipers, mock oranges, and Cherokee roses.

The Owens-Thomas House is one of several museum houses in Savannah.

Directions

From I-95, take Exit 17 (I-16) and travel east until the interstate dead-ends into Montgomery Street. Be prepared to make an almost immediate right turn onto West Charlton Street. Travel past Pulaski Square and Madison Square. The house is on the left at the corner as you approach Lafayette Square.

Tips

The last tour of the house begins at 4:30 p.m., but don't wait to take this final tour. You will want to ask questions and take your time in the garden and the gift shop, located in the carriage house at the rear of the property.

Accessibility

The house offers only limited access for disabled persons. The garden is accessible, but care should be taken on the walkway, as some areas are uneven.

Side Trips

The area boasts six other gardens and the historic Savannah squares (see pages 124–45 and 150–55).

Once used as the stable yard, the Parterre Garden was added in the 1950s.

SAVANNAH SQUARES

Address

Park and Tree Commission
P.O. Box 1027
Savannah, Georgia 31402-1027
912-651-6610

Hours

The squares are always open.

Fees

None

History

In February 1733, General James Edward Oglethorpe and one hundred colonists landed at Yamacraw Bluff on the Savannah River. Within a few days of arriving in the newly formed Georgia colony, Oglethorpe laid out the city of Savannah, beginning with Johnson Square, named for South Carolina governor Robert Johnson. Oglethorpe's simple plan was designed around common areas used for social or religious meetings and open-air markets. These rectangular units were called *wards* and were divided into quadrangles. Each quadrangle contained one-fourth of the central square, one trust lot, and ten house lots, called *tythings*. Trust lots were the largest and were reserved for public buildings. Some scholars believe Oglethorpe's design can be traced to one used for Beijing, China.

Part of the plan for founding Georgia was to buffer the upper twelve colonies from the Spanish-held territory of Florida. In its early years, Savannah was heavily fortified to withstand possible attacks from the south. As Savannah grew, citizens moved to outlying areas, and the squares assumed an important role in the protection of these colonists. Oglethorpe assigned them a particular ward to which they would come in the event of attack.

From 1733 until after the American Revolution, Savannah remained a city with only six squares, but by 1851, all twenty-four squares were laid out. The squares have withstood nearly every conceivable threat. Hurricanes, floods, fires, and even General William T. Sherman

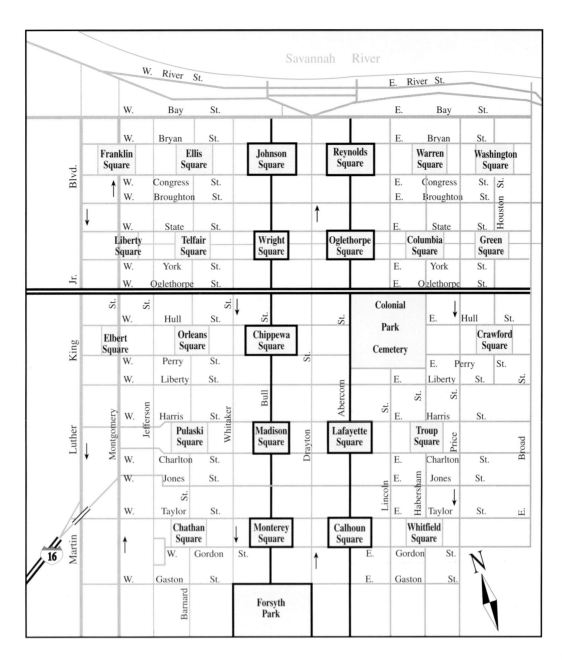

were unable to destroy the twenty-four jewels in Savannah's priceless necklace. Only progress, a man-made plague which roared into the city disguised as automobiles, marred four of the gems. Ellis Square, laid out in 1733 and dedicated to Henry Ellis, second Royal governor of Savannah, was the location of the City Market. In 1954, the market was demolished and the square turned into a parking lot. Liberty Square, honoring the "Sons of Liberty" who fought during the Revolutionary War, was lost to a roadway, as were Franklin Square, named for Benjamin Franklin, and Elbert Square, named for General Samuel Elbert, a former governor of Georgia. Ellis Square is only a memory and Elbert Square is a shadow of its former self, but Franklin and Liberty Squares have risen from the dead. Today, the remaining twenty-two squares stand as testaments to a prosperous past and a future that will preserve them as National Historic Civil Engineering Landmarks.

Pulaski Square, laid out in 1837, was named for Count Casimir Pulaski, who died during the siege of Savannah in 1779.

Size

22 squares of varying size within Savannah's historic district

Features

Canopied by oak trees dripping with moss, decorated with millions of azalea blooms, and accented with seasonal plantings, Savannah's squares are like precious gems strung together with a strong historical thread. The squares, beautifully maintained by the city, reflect Savannah's love affair with history but can confuse the uninitiated visitor. Just because a square bears an individual's name doesn't necessarily mean the statue or monument at the square honors that person. For example, Johnson Square, named for the South Carolina governor who assisted the new Georgia colony, has a monument to and the grave of Revolutionary War general Nathanael Greene in its center. Greene Square, named for the general, is nicely landscaped, but there's no monument to General Greene. Likewise, Polish count Casimir Pulaski has a square named in his honor, but the monument to his memory is in Monterey Square. Visitors can enjoy other public park features like benches, gazebos, and fountains while wondering why General James Oglethorpe's bronze statue is in Chippewa Square and not Oglethorpe Square.

Madison Square, named for
President James Madison,
was laid out in 1837.

Directions

From I-95, take Exit 17 (I-16) and travel east until the interstate dead-ends into Montgomery Street. Montgomery Street, sometimes called the "Street of Lost Squares," is a good place to start your driving tour. Refer to the map on page 151 for the location of the squares.

Laid out in 1734, Lower New Square
was renamed Reynolds Square in
1758 for a Georgia governor.

Tips

The wide variety of plantings in the squares
makes for an enjoyable visit at any time of the
year. Remember that parking can be difficult
and that a number of the squares are surrounded
by private residences.

Accessibility

All of Savannah's squares are accessible to the
disabled, as they can be viewed from a vehicle.
Paved sidewalks also provide easy access.

Side Trips

There are seven gardens in the Savannah area
(see pages 124–49).

Georgia Southern Botanical Garden

Address

Georgia Southern University
Landrum Box 8042
Statesboro, Georgia 30460-8042
912-871-1114

Hours

Open Monday through Friday from 9:00 a.m. to
6:00 p.m. and Sunday from 2:00 p.m. to 5:00 p.m.
Closed on Saturday.

Fees

None

History

Seeds for this small garden were sown in 1985,
when the longtime home of Dan and
Catharine Bland was bequeathed to Georgia
Southern University for use as a botanical garden and wildlife preserve.

Dan Edgar Bland was born on the farm now
known as Georgia Southern Botanical Garden.
He married Catharine O'Neal in 1916, shortly
after they both graduated from the First District
Agricultural School, now Georgia Southern
University. Dan brought Catharine to live on
the fifty-eight acres of the family farm his father
had given him as a graduation present. An old
tenant farmhouse, renovated and expanded,
became and remained their home until their
deaths, hers in 1983 and his in 1985.

For more than sixty years, Dan and Catharine
made a respectable living by selling a variety of
farm-fresh products such as pecans, pears, corn,
potatoes, hay, syrup, vegetables, hogs, cows,
chickens, butter, and eggs. The land sustained
the Blands throughout their lives, kept them
self-sufficient, and provided their customers
with produce almost year-round. As the years
passed, Dan and Catharine subdivided and sold
off parts of their farm, eventually retaining only
eight acres. These eight acres were left to the

university upon Dan's death. The university was the beneficiary of not only the property but of the love two people had for the land, the environment, and the school which provided them the knowledge that enabled them to live life on their own terms.

Size
10 acres

Features
The focus of this relatively new garden is on plants native to the Southeast, particularly those indigenous to the coastal plain of Georgia. There is a lot packed into these ten urban acres, and more is to come since the adoption of an updated master plan in 1993. Featured at the garden is the Enhanced Mixed Pine and Hardwood Zone, a naturalized woodland area displaying species known to thrive in a forest understory environment. There is also the Heritage Zone, which features the Bland Cottage and original farm buildings. The cottage is a multipurpose building housing a visitor center, a gift shop, a classroom, and administrative offices. Garden areas featured are the Butterfly Border, the Tully Pennington Camellia Collection, and the Children's Vegetable Garden. Future additions will include the Herb Garden, the Sandhill Habitat Garden, the Pond and Marsh Garden, the Pitcher Plant Bog, a savanna, the Shrub Zone, and the Children's Garden, which will be located near the Enhanced Mixed Pine and Hardwood Zone and will highlight plants children enjoy. There will also be a hands-on sculpture experience for children.

Directions
From I-16, take Exit 26 (GA 67) and travel north for 11.5 miles; GA 67 becomes Fair Road. Turn left onto Martha's Lane, then right onto Georgia Avenue. Take the next right, Bland Avenue. The entrance is on the right at 0.1 mile.

Tips
If your interest is native plants growing in their natural setting, this is the place for you. Reminiscent of a turn-of-the-century farmstead, this garden is experiencing expansion and improvements.

Accessibility
The gift shop is accessible to disabled persons. Designated parking and other improvements are being made to the garden.

Side Trips
Located 20 miles west is Metter, home to Guido Gardens (pages 94–97). Sixty miles east are the Savannah gardens and the historic Savannah squares (pages 124–55).

PANOLA MOUNTAIN STATE CONSERVATION PARK

Address

2600 Georgia 155, SW
Stockbridge, Georgia 30281-5236
770-389-7801

Hours

Open daily September 15 through April 14 from 7:00 a.m. to 6:00 p.m. and April 15 through September 14 from 7:00 a.m. to 9:00 p.m. The Interpretive Center is open Tuesday through Friday from 9:00 a.m. to 5:00 p.m. and Saturday and Sunday from noon to 5:00 p.m. Closed on Monday (except major holidays), Thanksgiving, Christmas, and New Year's Day.

Fees

A fee is charged for parking except on Wednesday.

History

Established in 1971 as Georgia's first conservation park, Panola Mountain State Conservation Park was originally a private summer retreat for the Yarborough family, who sold it to the Georgia State Conservancy in 1967. The conservancy, with the help and financial support of the Nature Conservancy, held the property until 1969, during which time the state of Georgia acquired the funds necessary to buy the 472 acres. This initial tract included a 100-acre granite dome believed to be the only exposed granite mountain in the Southeast left untouched by man. Subsequent land acquisitions facilitated by the Georgia Heritage Trust in 1974 and 1976 added 155 acres to the park. In 1991, additional land acquired through Preservation 2000 expanded the park to its present size.

Size

633 acres

Features

The most striking feature of the park is the granite mountain, which provides an unparalleled view of the surrounding area. Rocky outcrops and forests of hardwoods and pines add to the splendor of the park. Other features include a spring-fed pond, picnic shelters, a playground, and the Interpretive Center. The park's four trails are a 1-mile exercise trail, two self-guided trails—one 0.75 mile in length and the other 1.25 miles in length—and a 3.5-mile guided trail. This latter trail, offered only on weekends, leads to the granite mountain.

Directions

From I-20, take Exit 37 and travel south for 3.7 miles to Panola Road. Panola Road dead-ends at Snapfinger Road (GA 155). Turn left (south) onto Snapfinger Road and travel 2.5 miles. The entrance to the park is on the left.

Tips

A variety of programs is scheduled throughout the year, including two wildflower walks, one in the spring and another in the fall. You may wish to call ahead for a schedule of events. Also, call ahead if you plan to take the 3.5-mile guided hike to the mountain. Ranger-led programs tailored for groups should be scheduled in advance. A minimal fee is charged for ranger-led programs and guided hikes.

Accessibility

Designated parking is available at the park. The Interpretive Center and the restrooms are accessible to disabled persons.

Side Trips

The William H. Reynolds Nature Preserve (pages 104–5) is about 20 miles southwest in Morrow. The Melvin L. Newman Wetlands Center (pages 70–71) is about 30 miles south in Hampton.

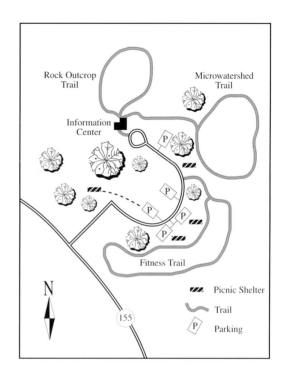

BIRDSONG NATURE CENTER

Address

2106 Meridian Road
Thomasville, Georgia 31792-0417
912-377-4408

Hours

Open Wednesday and Friday from 9:00 a.m. to noon, Saturday from 9:00 a.m. to 2:00 p.m., and Sunday from 1:00 p.m. to 5:00 p.m. Closed on all major holidays.

Fees

Yes. Discounts are available for children and members.

History

Originally named Birdsong Plantation, the nature preserve was at one time a working plantation. Farmed for nearly one hundred years by four generations of the Dickey family, Birdsong Plantation was no more than a dream when Shadrach and Susannah Dickey brought their young son William from their South Carolina home to the town of Duncanville in 1830. Duncanville, known today as Thomasville, was Shadrach Dickey's home until his death in 1847. In 1851, William received his share of his father's estate: 250 acres and some personal property, which included slaves and livestock. Dickey prospered, and the plantation grew to 565 acres by 1903.

In 1938, it was purchased from the Dickey family by Ed and Betty Komarek. The Komareks, both dedicated naturalists, worked diligently for nearly fifty years to turn the overworked land into a wildlife sanctuary. In 1981, they opened Birdsong Nature Center in an effort to teach the importance of conserving natural resources and to demonstrate the benefits of effective land management. The center was established as a nonprofit organization in 1986.

Size
565 acres

Features
The Komareks have worked something just short of a miracle in developing the six acres around the old farmhouse into a lushly landscaped haven. Gone are the views of a dusty, barren chicken yard. Today, the grounds around the house, which is listed on the National Register of Historic Places, have been planted with native plants to provide food for birds and butterflies. Some varieties of butterflies use the plants as hosts for their eggs. Inside the house is the very popular Bird Window, a floor-to-ceiling observation window which allows visitors to enjoy an up-close experience of bird-watching. Located on the grounds are 12 miles of trails; most trails are 0.5- to 2-mile loops. Bluebird Trail, one of the most popular, features thirty-four strategically placed bluebird nesting boxes. Other trails meander through the various preserve habitats. Trail maps are available at the center, which offers a variety of nature-oriented programs to the public.

Directions
From I-75, take Exit 4 (US 84) and travel west 37.5 miles to the Thomasville city limits, where US 84 becomes US 84 Business. From US 84 Business, take US 319 South for 13 miles to GA 93. Turn right, travel 1 mile to Meridian Road, and turn left. The entrance to the center is on the left at 3.8 miles.

Tips
Plan to visit either from January through May, when the birds are most active, or from June through November, when the butterflies are active. It is advisable to call ahead for a program listing, as some programs are open to the public but may be scheduled at times when the center is not normally open. On the last Sunday in October, the center hosts its annual Jubilee, complete with live music, crafts, nature walks, and programs covering a variety of subjects.

Accessibility
The trails are wheelchair-accessible. Some disabled individuals may require assistance to access the house.

Side Trips
Thomasville Rose Garden (pages 162–63) is nearby. Located 45 miles east of Thomasville is Valdosta, home of The Crescent (pages 164–67).

THOMASVILLE
ROSE GARDEN

Address

Destination Thomasville Tourism Authority
P.O. Box 1540
Thomasville, Georgia 31799-1540
912-225-3919

Hours

Open daily from sunrise to sunset

Fees

None

History

Since the 1920s, Thomasville has been known as the "City of Roses," inspired by the success of Thomasville Rose Nurseries. Peter J. Hjort, a Danish immigrant, started the nursery in 1898 and printed its first catalog in 1921. Three generations later, the business was shipping plants and garden-related products to all parts of the United States. In 1953, the nursery became the site for an All-American Rose Selections trial garden. These gardens evaluate new rose introductions for hardiness, disease resistance, and overall appeal to the average gardener. In 1994, after ninety-six years, the nursery closed its doors. Since the town's only public rose garden was gone, local government decided the "City of Roses" needed a municipal rose garden and contracted with Thomasville Landscape Company to handle the job.

Size

½ acre

Features

Located within sight of Cherokee Lake, the all-new Thomasville Rose Garden begins blooming near the middle of April, depending upon the spring weather. The roses are usually in full bloom by the first of May, providing the perfect setting for the newly constructed gazebo.

Directions

From I-75, take Exit 4 (US 84 West) and travel 37.5 miles into Thomasville, where US 84 becomes US 84 Business. From where the highway changes names, it is 8.3 miles to Covington Street; turn right. The garden is on the left at 0.1 mile.

Tips

The roses begin blooming in the middle of April and continue through November. In April, the city goes rose crazy with its annual Rose Show and Festival. Reservations are required, so write for a program.

Hybrid tea roses, recognized as a distinct rose type in 1867, can be found in the newly planted garden.

Accessibility

Designated parking and paved walkways provide easy access for disabled persons.

Side Trips

Birdsong Nature Center (pages 160–61) is also located in Thomasville. The Crescent (pages 164–67) is 55 miles east in Valdosta.

THE CRESCENT

Address

904 North Patterson Street
P.O. Box 2423
Valdosta, Georgia 31604-2423
912-244-6747

Hours

The grounds are open year-round. The house and support buildings are open Monday through Friday from 2:00 p.m. to 5:00 p.m. and by appointment; they are closed on Saturday and Sunday and during major holidays and private events.

Fees

Donations are accepted for house tours.

History

Patterson Street in Valdosta boasts a collection of beautifully preserved and restored houses, part of an aging but rather affluent neighborhood. Small businesses began to infiltrate the neighborhood, once known as Million-aires Row, in the early to mid-1950s as old families died out and houses fell into disrepair. Stately old homes were being turned into insurance companies, law offices, and the like, forever changing the complexion of the neighborhood.

Progress seemed to be the fate of all the old homes on Millionaires Row, including that of Senator William S. West. The Crescent, as it was called because of its distinctive crescent-shaped front porch, was built in 1898 by West. The once-palatial Crescent was purchased in the early 1950s by local businessmen and was scheduled to be torn down and replaced by a gas station.

The thought of never being able to drive by The Crescent and see the old oak trees shading the play yard was more than Mrs. T. H. Smith could bear. Mrs. Smith, an active member of the Holly Garden Club of Valdosta, refused to allow one of the city's most distinctive landmarks to fall to the bulldozer's blade. She enlisted the aid of Mrs. Leonard Mederer and Mrs. R. B.

Thirteen columns represent-
ing the original colonies grace
the crescent-shaped portico.

Whitehead in saving The Crescent. Their plan was to rally local garden clubs around the idea of establishing The Crescent as a headquarters for the city's various garden clubs.

Establishing a headquarters had been a topic of garden club meetings, but nothing definite had ever been decided until the prospect of losing part of Valdosta's heritage loomed large. The ladies of the garden clubs mobilized. Beginning with only five hundred dollars in their treasury, they worked hard to raise the money to eventually buy the property.

Once the garden clubs owned The Crescent, the next project for the ladies was to restore and improve the house and the surrounding garden. Originally, the grounds were very informal, in keeping with the wishes of Mrs. West, the former Ora Lee Cranford, who wanted a place for her children and their friends to play. Most of the houses along Millionaires Row boasted a formal front garden reserved for entertaining and meditation, but The Crescent was not most houses, and the owners were not ordinary people. William and Ora Lee West had loved children.

The aura of a family home is what the ladies of the garden clubs wanted to preserve.

The task of implementing such a plan went to R. J. Drexel. Drexel's plan called for preserving the original front landscape, which consisted of oak trees planted by Senator West and native azaleas. It also called for developing a formal landscape at the rear of the house in order to showcase the talents of the seven garden clubs responsible for rescuing the lovely old Crescent.

The Garden Center Headquarters, chartered in 1952, assembled under one roof the Amaryllis Garden Club, the Azalea Garden Club, the Camellia Garden Club, the Dogwood Garden Club, the Holly Garden Club, the Magnolia Garden Club, and the Town and Country Garden Club. Each club maintains its separate identity, but all call The Crescent home.

Size
¾ acre

Features
The house is clearly the main attraction of the complex, but the seven garden clubs and their talented gardeners do a splendid job with the limited space allotted to them. The small garden features a variety of plants incorporated into a basic formal design. All plants throughout the garden are clearly marked. There is a small chapel at one end of the long, rectangular garden and a community-use building at the other end. A fountain in the center adds the pleasant sound of running water, and an arbor along the back displays vine plants which enjoy the climate of southern Georgia.

Directions
From I-75, take Exit 4 (US 84 East) and travel 2.3 miles to Toombs Street. Turn left, travel 0.6 mile to Gordon Street, and turn right. The entrance to The Crescent is on the left in the middle of the block.

Tips
The garden is small yet beautifully planted and well tended. Allow approximately an hour to tour the house and wander though the garden. The Crescent is a popular community attraction, so call ahead to find out if the facility is scheduled to be used for a private event during the time you plan to visit.

Accessibility
Most of the garden can be seen from a vehicle. Some individuals may require assistance on the brick pathways. The first floor of the house is accessible to disabled persons.

Side Trips
Located 45 miles west of Valdosta is Thomasville, home of Birdsong Nature Center (pages 160–61) and Thomasville Rose Garden (pages 162–63).

BIBLIOGRAPHY

Adams, Kevin, and Marty Casstevens. *Wildflowers of the Southern Appalachians: How to Photograph and Identify Them*. Winston-Salem, NC: John F. Blair, Publisher, 1996.

The Antique Rose Emporium. Dahlonega, GA: Antique Rose Emporium.

Apple Corps, Inc. *Natural Selections: A Guide to Great Science and Nature Outings in Georgia*. Atlanta, GA: Apple Corps, Inc., 1993.

Biggers, Edna et al., eds. *Berry Trails: An Historic and Contemporary Guide to Berry College*. 2d ed. Mount Berry, GA: Berry Woman's Club, 1987.

Brickell, Christopher et al., eds. *The American Horticultural Society Encyclopedia of Gardening*. New York: Dorling Kindersley, 1994.

A Brief History of the Bamboo Farm. Savannah, GA: Coastal Area Extension Center.

Bull, John, and John Farrand, Jr. *The Audubon Society Field Guide to North American Birds: Eastern Region*. New York: Alfred A. Knopf, 1993.

Cairns, Thomas, ed. *Modern Roses 10: The Comprehensive List of Roses of Historical and Botanical Importance Including All Modern International Rose Registrations*. Shreveport, LA: American Rose Society, 1993.

Cofer, Carl H. *The Barnsley Gardens Story*. 1992.

Cooper, Emmeline King, and Polly Wylly Cooper. *A Visitor's Guide to Savannah: A Coastal Cities Guidebook*. Charleston, SC: Wyrick & Company, 1995.

Farrington, Edward I. *The Gardener's Travel Book*. New York: Oxford University Press, 1949.

The Fred Hamilton Rhododendron Garden. Lookout Mountain, GA: Georgia Mountain Fair.

Gordon, Arthur. "The Guido Story." *Guideposts Magazine* (March 1984): 38-41.

Hayward, Robert. *Fernbank*. Atlanta, GA: Fernbank Science Center.

Tickseed sunflower (Bidens aristosa) *is a common road-side wildflower.*

History of Massee Lane Gardens, Headquarters of the American Camellia Society. Fort Valley, GA: Massee Lane Gardens.

History of Vines Botanical Gardens. Loganville, GA: Vines Botanical Gardens.

Hjort Family. Thomasville, GA: Thomas County Library.

Jones, Charles C., Jr. *Jones' Memorial History of Augusta.* Spartanburg, SC: Reprint Publishing Company, 1980.

Marye, Florence. *Garden History of Georgia, 1733-1933: Georgia Bicentennial Edition.* 1933. Reprint, Atlanta, GA: Peachtree Garden Club, 1976.

Melvin L. Newman Wetlands Center: Come Take a Walk Through Our Wetlands. Hampton, GA: Clayton County Water Authority.

Miller, Everitt L., and J. S. Cohen. *The American Garden Guidebook: A Traveler's Guide to Extraordinary Beauty Along the Beaten Path.* New York: M. Evans and Company, 1987.

Mitchell, William. *Gardens of Georgia.* Atlanta, GA: Peachtree Publishers, 1989.

Mitchell, William R., Jr. *Classic Savannah: History, Homes, and Gardens.* Savannah, GA: Golden Coast Publishing Company, 1987.

Niering, William A., and Nancy C. Olmstead. *The Audubon Society Field Guide to North American Wildflowers: Eastern Region.* New York: Alfred A. Knopf, 1992.

Panola Mountain State Conservation Park. Stockbridge, GA: Georgia Department of Natural Resources.

Ray, Mary Helen, and Robert P. Nicholls. *The Traveler's Guide to American Gardens.* Chapel Hill, NC: University of North Carolina Press, 1988.

Schubert, Paul. *Cason Callaway of Blue Springs.* Atlanta, GA: Foote & Davies, 1964.

Shultz, Gladys Denny, and Daisy Gordon Lawrence. *Lady from Savannah: The Life of Juliette Low.* New York: J. B. Lippincott Company, 1958.

Sieg, Chan. *The Squares: An Introduction to Savannah.* Norfolk, VA: Donning, 1984.

Strickland, Rita. "A Garden for the Nation's First Garden Club." *Southern Living* 27 (March 1992): 10sc-11sc.

Turner, Charlotte. *The Cator Woolford Property: Gardens and Grounds Restoration Proposal.* Atlanta, GA: Reach, Inc., 1994.

Waldorf, G. B. *A History of Birdsong Plantation.* Thomasville, GA: Birdsong Nature Center, 1991.

INDEX